BONDED BY BATTLE

BONDED BY BATTLE

The Powerful Friendships
Of Military Dogs and Soldiers

FROM THE CIVIL WAR TO OPERATION IRAQI FREEDOM

Nancy Roe Pimm

QUINDARO

Quindaro Press · Kansas City, Missouri

Text copyright © 2017 by Nancy Roe Pimm

Publisher's Cataloging-In-Publication Data
(Prepared by The Donohue Group, Inc.)

Names: Pimm, Nancy Roe.
Title: Bonded by battle : the powerful friendships of military dogs
and soldiers : from the Civil War to Operation Iraqi Freedom / Nancy
Roe Pimm.
Description: Kansas City, Missouri : Quindaro Press, [2017] |
Interest age level: 12 and up. | Includes bibliographical references
and index. | Summary: "A history from the Civil War onward of the
partnership between military dogs and their human companions.
Describes the evolving relationship as the dogs' skills are discovered
and exploited by their handlers, and the U.S. military's changing
policy toward the dogs." — Provided by publisher.
Identifiers: ISBN 978-0-9764434-6-9
Subjects: LCSH: Dogs—War use—United States—History—
Juvenile literature. | Working dogs—United States—History—Juvenile
literature. | Human-animal relationships—United States—History—
Juvenile literature. | CYAC: Dogs—War use—United States—
History. | Working dogs—United States—History. | Human-animal
relationships—United States—History.
Classification: LCC UH100 .P56 2017 | DDC 355.4/240973--dc23

Library of Congress Control Number: 2017935341

Published by Quindaro Press
3808 Genessee Street
Kansas City, Missouri 64111
www.quindaropress.com

2 4 6 8 10 9 7 5 3 1

TABLE OF CONTENTS

This book is dedicated to all of our veterans past and present, the two-legged soldiers as well as the four-legged. The soldiers in my family tree were not dog handlers, but they bravely served our country in times of war — my great-great grandfather
Michael Dougherty (Civil War),
my grandfather Russel Jacob Roe (World War I),
my father Edward Joseph Roe (World War II),
my uncle Donald Joseph Roe (the Korean War),
my cousin John Roe (Vietnam War),
and my nephew Edward Joseph Roe
(Operation Iraqi Freedom).

In memory of Alissa Trucco —
rest in peace, my fellow book lover, horse lover,
dog lover,
and family friend.

INTRODUCTION:
IT TAKES TWO

He is your friend, your defender, your dog.
You are his life, his love, his leader.
He will be yours faithful and true,
To the last beat of his heart.
You owe it to him to be worthy of such devotion.
Anonymous

There is something about a dog. Forever loyal, they offer unconditional love. They greet their favorite human with glowing eyes, wagging tails, and wiggling bodies. And the bond between man and dog is as long as it is strong. How long? Archeologists discovered fossilized remains of cave dwellers and dogs buried side by side. Scientists believe that dogs protected our prehistoric ancestors in times of danger, assisted them in the hunt for food, and even followed them into combat.

In Egypt, wall writings approximately 6,000 years old portray warriors gripping the leashes of vicious dogs leaping on the enemy. Temple walls in Iraq depict huge mastiff battle dogs wearing spiked iron collars. All manner of armies — Persian, Assyrian, Babylonian — sent dogs out to the front lines to take down their enemies' horses and force infantrymen to lower their shields, exposing them to attack.

During the Peloponnesian War (431-404 BCE), a detachment of Greek warriors approached the citadel of Corinth as their enemy lay sleeping inside its walls. Having returned from a great victory, the Corinthians had celebrated late into the night. They would be easy prey for an ambush, or so the Greeks thought. But as these intruders stormed the citadel, fifty wide-awake warriors were waiting for them — the Corinthian canine corps stood guard at the perimeter of the city. As the Greeks approached, the dogs attacked. Forty-nine of the fifty dogs died at the hands of the enemy soldiers, but one dog escaped and fled to town to wake the sleeping soldiers. After a bloody but victorious defense, the city ordered a silver collar for their canine savior with the inscription, "Soter, defender and preserver of Corinth." A marble monument was erected to honor the forty-nine fallen soldier dogs.

During the battle of Vercellae in 101 BCE, the Teuton women led packs of dogs wearing protective armor against the Romans. Although it was a lost cause, the dogs kept the victors at bay for hours. The Romans took notice and soon

This Roman statue from the 2nd century BCE shows a Molossian hound, also known as a mastiff. These large dogs were used by the Roman and Greek armies, both to guard and to attack.

had trained their own canine formations to run underneath enemy horses. The dogs, clad in body armor that bristled with razor-sharp spikes, caused the horses to throw their mounts. When the enemy soldiers hit the ground, the huge mastiff-type dogs pounced. Five centuries later, giant Molossian dogs serving Attila the Hun's army could play both offense and defense. Encased in protective plates, the canine warriors stood guard against sneak attacks and also joined their human companions in battle.

Little is said in these ancient accounts of the relationship between dogs and soldiers. But anyone who has experienced the fierce devotion of a dog surely knows what that bond must have been like. During the Seven Years' War (1756-1763), the Prussian king Frederick the Great reportedly said, "The more I see of men, the better I like my dog."[1]

Like the great generals before him, Napoleon Bonaparte understood the tactical importance of dogs in war. He posted sentries to the walls surrounding Alexandria, Egypt, when his French army occupied that city. Their barks served as an early warning system. But Napoleon also witnessed the emotional side of dogs, the comfort and compassion they bring to the fields of suffering and death.

While inspecting the carnage after the Battle of Castiglione in 1796, he encountered a dog whining and licking the hand of his human companion who lay before him lifeless. As Napoleon approached, the dog — not knowing or caring that this man was the emperor of France — barked insistently, pleading with him to come to the aid of his soldier. Later, Napoleon would write the following:

"Perhaps it was the spirit of the time and place that affected me. But I assure you no occurrence of any of my other battlefields impressed me so keenly. I halted on my tour to gaze on the spectacle and reflect on its meaning. This soldier, I realized, must have had friends at home and in his regiment; yet lay there deserted by all except his dog. . . . I had looked on, unmoved, at battles which decide the future of nations. Tearless, I had given orders which brought death to thousands. Yet here I was stirred, profoundly stirred, stirred to tears. And by what? By the grief of one dog."[2]

Today, canines are used in combat operations as never before serving the American armed forces. These four-footed soldiers — officially called military working dogs — not only protect as guard dogs at military bases, but they also alert soldiers to hidden explosives in buildings and vehicles and beneath roads. Some leap out of airplanes and free-fall 10,000 feet with their handlers, or are strapped to their handlers' backs as they fast-rope out of helicopters and drop into remote battle zones. Fitted with bulletproof vests, they become live remote control action figures responding to commands they hear in their earbuds, and sending back night-vision video from head-mounted cameras.

"The working dog is a weapon system that is resilient, compact, easily deployable, and can move fast when needed," says Air Force Master Sergeant Antonio Rodriguez, who has overseen more than one hundred military working dog teams. "Nothing compares."[3] Former commander of

United States forces in Afghanistan General David Petraeus agrees. "The capability they bring to the fight cannot be replicated by man or machine," he said. [4]

Along with the latest high-tech gear strapped to their bodies, their natural sensory powers serve as built-in weapons. Start with those hard-working noses. The number of smell receptors in a dog's nose ranges from 125 million to 300 million, compared to as few as five or six million in a human nose.

While humans see with their eyes, dogs "see" with their noses. A dog inhales through its nostrils and exhales out of the slits located on each side of its nose. This swirling motion of inhaled and exhaled air gives the dog a steady stream of air and new odors. "When airflow enters the nose it splits into two different paths, one for olfaction and one for respiration," said Brent Craven, a bioengineer at Pennsylvania State University. [5]

Dogs also have a better sense of smell because the part of their brain that is devoted to analyzing scents is forty times larger than a human's. While the olfactory area of our brain is about the size of a postage stamp, if you could unfold the olfactory area of a dog's brain it would be as large as 60 square inches, about the size of a piece of paper. This makes for a nose that scientists have estimated to be 10,000 to 100,000 times more sensitive than human noses. [6]

Mike Ritland, a former Navy SEAL who now cares for retired military working dogs, explains it this way. "If you and I walk into the kitchen and there's a pot of beef stew on the counter, you and I smell beef stew," he said. "A dog

*A bomb-detecting dog and his handler on the island of
Guam during World War II.*

smells potatoes, carrots, beef, onion, celery, gravy, flour
— each and every individual component of everything
that's in that beef stew. And they can separate every one
of those. You can't hide anything from them."[7]

Then there are those marvelous ears. It is believed
they can hear sounds precisely from a quarter mile away,
including high frequency sounds that human ears can't
pick up. With more than eighteen muscles, a dog can control the movement of its ear to capture sound and locate

from where it's coming. It can hear the far-off click of a rifle in time to alert the soldiers who rely on them. [8]

But perhaps the most remarkable quality of dogs is not the nose or ears, it's their heart. They give it up completely to their handler — the soldier who becomes the dog's trainer and constant companion, on and off the battlefield. They are obedient to every command given, even to making the ultimate sacrifice for their handler. And the handler returns the devotion in full.

Throughout their deployment, handlers treat their canine companions like humans. They read books and letters to them, or just talk to their trusted partners for hours on end. "They get to be like your best friends," said Staff Sgt. Jason Winge. "You can tell them anything and they act like they're listening." [9] The bond intensifies further on the battlefield. Tom Hewitt recalls that he and his dog Paper were inseparable during their tour of Vietnam. "That dog was like my hand. If I move my hand, I don't have to tell my fingers what to do. That dog became so much a part of me that, if he wasn't there, it was like I was missing a hand." [10]

In this book we will travel through history alongside canine warriors and "their" soldiers as they served their country and saved countless lives. From the mascot dogs of the Civil War and the world wars to the new breed of military working dogs that served from the Vietnam War to the Operation Iraqi Freedom, these stories show that humans and dogs fighting side by side form an unbreakable bond that is a force to be reckoned with.

Army Rangers and a military working dog pause during a nighttime combat mission in Afghanistan.

CHAPTER ONE

DOG JACK

Nearly every regiment of the Civil War (1861-1865) had some type of animal mascot that ate, slept, and went to battle with the soldiers. The 3rd Louisiana Confederates had a donkey who repeatedly tried to sleep in the tent of the commanding officer. A tame bear lumbered along with the 12th Wisconsin Volunteers as they marched to Missouri. Robert E. Lee's pet hen rewarded the general with a fresh egg under his cot every morning. "Old Abe," a bald eagle named in honor of President Lincoln, came to symbolize the United States of America. A sheep named Dick, a pig named Jeff Davis, and a camel named Douglas also served as mascots.

While most regiments chose their mascots, the mascot of the 102nd Regiment of Pennsylvania Volunteers chose them. One day in late 1860 or early 1861 a bull terrier mix with a brown patch of fur over his left eye wandered into the Niagara Fire Engine House on Pennsylvania Avenue in Pittsburgh. Perhaps someone gave him food, because the dog decided to stay and was given a name — Dog Jack.

Some time later, the dog's leg was broken. There were conflicting stories. Did one of the firefighters kick this uninvited guest in an attempt to make him leave? Or did the dog hurt himself while racing the firefighters to a blazing building? However it happened, one of the men took pity on the injured dog and set its broken leg in a splint.[1]

Dog Jack regained his strength, but his leg healed crookedly. One day as he limped about the firehouse, a much larger dog attacked him. Dog Jack fought back with incredible ferocity, earning new respect from all of the fire fighters. Their house became his home. He never missed a meal again.

Every time the fire alarm sounded, he barked excitedly. According to the firehouse chaplain, Alexander M. Stewart, "Jack was always in high glee when the fire bell sounded, ran with the shouting company, and rendered all the assistance possible."[2] His "assistance" consisted mostly of running up and down the street making a commotion.

When the entire Niagara fire company enlisted in the Civil War, their gimpy, noisy bull terrier led the way. Instinctively Dog Jack only obeyed orders given by the men of Company F of the 102nd Regiment, Pennsylvania Volunteers.

Like a good soldier, he understood all of the bugle calls. In the heat of a battle, Dog Jack barked eagerly as he took the lead and charged straight to the front lines. Once the fighting ended, he roamed the battlefield comforting the wounded. When he came upon a dead or dying soldier, Dog Jack simply lay down beside him.

This photograph of Dog Jack is dated 1865, but was actually taken before his disappearance in December 1864.

On July 1, 1862, at the battle of Malvern Hill, Virginia, a bullet pierced his shoulder and back. His fellow soldiers carried their wounded warrior to the hospital tent with tears streaming down their faces. Their canine companion hovered between life and death, but finally Dog Jack returned to the battlefield amongst the cheers of his fellow soldiers.

The battles ahead proved to be the bloodiest. Company F fought their way through the Wilderness campaign, the battle of Spotsylvania, and the siege of Petersburg in Virginia. The 102nd Pennsylvania battled nearly everywhere in the eastern theater of the war.

At Salem Church, Virginia, on May 3, 1863, the Confederate army captured ninety-four Union soldiers and one canine commando. Jack remained a prisoner of war, and by all accounts he kept his cheerful disposition while in captivity. He spent most of his time wagging his tail, licking faces, and lifting the spirits of his fellow prisoners.

In the fall of 1863, perhaps for the first time ever, a canine soldier was swapped for a human soldier. After six months of confinement, Jack walked away a free dog. At Savage Station, Virginia, the Confederate soldiers captured Dog Jack again, but this time he managed to escape and find his way back to the Union lines.

The soldiers enjoyed a brief furlough from all of the fighting in August of 1864. They held a ball at Lafayette Hall in Pittsburgh and raised $75, which with the rate of inflation is equal to over $1,100 today. The men used all of the money to honor their soldier dog by purchasing a collar made of pure silver, with a medal of bravery attached.

Unfortunately, only four months later, on December 23, 1864, Dog Jack disappeared. Some speculate he died fending off a robber in pursuit of the silver collar.[3]

At the war's end, the men of the 102nd Pennsylvania commissioned a portrait of Dog Jack. It hangs in Soldiers and Sailors National Military Museum and Memorial in Pittsburgh, Pennsylvania, a tribute to the courage and devotion of one dog who became so much more than a mascot.

The Eagle Mascot

Early in 1861, a family in northern Wisconsin traded goods with the Flambeau Band of the Ojibwe Indians. The settlers came away with an eaglet. They kept the bird of prey as a pet until they offered it to Company C of the 8th Wisconsin Infantry. The regiment adopted the eagle as their mascot in the Civil War, naming it "Old Abe" in honor of President Lincoln. The 8th Wisconsin soon became known as the Eagle Regiment. When in battle, the men kept the bird tethered to a perch on top of a wooden pole. The bird flapped his feathers and screeched loudly before each battle. Confederates tried in vain to capture or kill "the Yankee buzzard." Three of his bearers were wounded in action, but "Old Abe" remained unharmed. The bird's fame spread throughout the North. He was used as an army recruitment tool and a popular song, "Old Abe the Battle Eagle," was written about him.[4]

The sale of thousands of photographs of "Old Abe" raised money for wounded soldiers and families of fallen soldiers. After the war, the eagle spent his days in a cage at the state capital in Madison, Wisconsin. In March 1881, after "Old Abe" died, state officials immediately had him stuffed and the popular bird went back on public display.[5]

"Old Abe"

Horses in the Civil War

Horses and the soldiers who rode on their backs often formed strong bonds in the battlefields. One of the best-known horses of the Civil War was Traveller, Gen. Robert E. Lee's beloved steed from champion stock in Greenbrier County, Virginia. Lee described him as "Confederate gray," and he sported a black mane and tail. Traveller was a hard-charging horse that rarely walked. The two remained together until Lee's death, when Traveller walked behind the hearse during the funeral procession. The horse is buried at Lee Chapel Museum, Lexington, Virginia.

Another Confederate soldier, Gen. Stonewall Jackson, strode upon a horse named Little Sorrel. The general purchased the ten-year-old gelding at Harpers Ferry, Virginia (now West Virginia). Jackson originally named him Fancy, and intended to give the horse to his wife, but the first time he sat on his back, they formed an immediate bond. Little Sorrel was so small that Jackson's feet almost dragged on the ground. The horse had amazing endurance and covered a mile in two and a half minutes. Although the other soldiers had trouble keeping up with the fleet-footed horse, Jackson found the horse's gait "as easy as the rocking of the cradle."[6] Little Sorrel bolted only once — when his rider was mortally wounded by gunfire from his own men, in the darkened woods of Chancellorsville on May 2, 1863.

Stonewall Jackson's horse Little Sorrel

CHAPTER TWO

RINTY

In Europe, local militias began breeding and training dogs for use in combat in the 1860s. The Germans established the world's very first military working dog academy in 1884. Located at Lechenich, the academy turned canine companions into tools of the national army. At first they were used as sentries, guarding prisoners of war, and as messengers, dashing through no-man's land to deliver vital communications.

Then the Germans trained them as mercy dogs, also known as Red Cross dogs. These dogs carried medical supplies in saddlebags on their backs to wounded soldiers who lay on the battlefield. If the soldier was dying, the mercy dog would simply lie down by his side and provide comfort until he passed.

Other European countries followed in Germany's paw prints. Britain's Col. E.H. Richardson trained mercy dogs, search dogs, sentry dogs, and dogs that carried saddlebags full of messenger pigeons to the front line five times faster than a human soldier could.

Carrier Pigeons

If a message needed to get from military headquarters to the front lines, or vice versa, it was hard to beat a carrier pigeon. With their astonishing success rate of 95 percent, the messenger pigeons were so vital to the Allied efforts in World War I that the German army began training hawks and falcons to take them out.

One carrier pigeon in particular, named Cher Ami (French for "dear friend"), earned one of France's highest military honors, the Croix de Guerre, for her courage in delivering an important message through deadly enemy fire. She arrived at her destination a bloody mess, shot through the chest and blinded in one eye. One leg was hanging by a tendon. The message that Cher Ami delivered was responsible for saving 194 American soldiers trapped behind German lines.[1]

Cher Ami

With the outbreak of world war in 1914, an estimated sixteen million animals were pressed into service. Britain's Imperial Camel Corps had thousands of trusty steeds. Nearly one million horses were part of various cavalry units. Mules pulled carts and transported packed loads. Up in the air, thousands of carrier pigeons relayed vital messages to and fro.

At least 75,000 canine operatives were put to use in World War I (1914-1918). Dogs became more than a soldier's best friend. Some dogs lugged spools of telegraph wire on their backs as they traveled from trench to trench, laying down lines of communications between soldiers. Big dogs pulled ammunition on carts. Little dogs cleared the trenches of hundreds of thousands of rats.

Only the United States did not have a dog program in the war. Just as they had done in the Civil War fifty years earlier, American soldiers brought mascot dogs with them or adopted strays that they had found while marching across Europe.

One of the most famous canines of World War I never saw action in battle, either as a mascot or as a working dog. Lee Duncan, a corporal in the U.S. Army's 135th Aero Squadron, discovered the pup in the rubble of war-torn France. His name was Rin Tin Tin.

* * *

It was September 15, 1918, toward the end of the war, and Cpl. Duncan had orders to inspect the ruins of a German encampment in the French village of Fluiry to determine if it would make a good airstrip. Duncan was tromping

Breeder Max von Stephanitz developed the German shepherd in the late 1800s to be of service to police and military. The dogs quickly became known for their endurance, steadiness, and intelligence.

through miles and miles of trenches and barbed wire when he noticed a partially destroyed concrete building. Since it resembled a dog kennel, and Duncan loved dogs, he took a closer look.

The soldier came upon the unforgettable sight of at least twenty dead army dogs, some with messenger pigeon cages still strapped to their backs. As Duncan released the pigeons, he heard a whimpering noise. He followed the sound and discovered a female dog nursing five hungry puppies.

They were a breed of dog that almost no American had seen until the war — the German shepherd. Introduced by a breeder named Max von Stephanitz only twenty years earlier, they were highly valued for their intelligence and willingness to work hard. After some coaxing, Duncan piled the protective mother and her babies into his vehicle and drove back to base.

This German shepherd litter immediately held a special place in Duncan's heart, for he knew what it was like to be abandoned. His own father had deserted the family, leaving his mother alone and unable to fend for two young children. Desperate and out of options, she took her five-year-old son Lee and his two-year-old sister and left them in an orphanage.

Back at the base, Cpl. Duncan gave the mother and three babies to his fellow soldiers. He kept two puppies for himself, one male and one female. Lee named the girl Nanette and the boy Rin Tin Tin — the names of two popular dolls that were also considered good luck charms. From a German prisoner of war, Duncan learned that thousands of German shepherds had served in the war and were thought of as the country's official war dog.

His fellow soldiers, however, did not share his enthusiasm for Nanette and "Rinty." They wanted the dogs out of their barracks. So he took the pups to an empty barn nearby and moved in with them. Duncan spent all his free time training and playing with the German shepherds. Using a squeaky toy as a reward, he found them to be smart and easy to train.

When the war ended, many war dogs were treated as little more than surplus equipment and were abandoned or destroyed. The governments whose armies they had served thought it was too costly and difficult to bring them back home. Influenza had killed millions of soldiers, and people were worried about diseases the animals might be carrying.

But Duncan wasn't about to leave two-year-old Nanette and Rinty behind. In July 1919, he received orders to board the *F.J. Luckenbach*, which was sailing for New York. As he prepared to board the ship with the dogs, an officer stopped Duncan and explained that he would need special permission and paperwork. The officer warned him not to even think about smuggling the dogs — captains were known for heaving unwanted animals overboard.

Duncan did it anyway. As he later recalled, "I felt there was something about their lives that reminded me of my own life. They had crept right into that lonesome place in my life and had become a part of me."[1]

Luckily for him, the *Luckenbach*'s captain had no intention of separating Duncan from his beloved German

A promotional photo of movie star Rin Tin Tin from 1930. It is signed by Lee Duncan, who discovered "Rinty" as a pup abandoned in a kennel in war-torn France.

shepherds. After Rinty and Nanette were discovered, the captain directed Duncan to another officer who would help him get the necessary papers to bring the dogs across the ocean.

Rinty fared well on the fifteen-day voyage to America, but Nanette contracted pneumonia and died shortly after arriving in New York.

Duncan and Rinty boarded a train headed across the country to his home in California. There they found the sleepy town of Hollywood had come alive with the booming new business of entertainment. The war was over and people flocked to the movie theaters to see the latest silent films.

Stories of this new breed of dog were brought back to America by its veterans, and German shepherds began to grow in popularity. In 1922 Duncan got Rinty bit parts in two films, one of them as a wolf. By 1924, Rin Tin Tin was starring as himself. He became one of the biggest box office stars, human or canine, in the world.

After Rinty died in 1932, radio broadcasts across America were interrupted for the news. Duncan quickly trained one of Rinty's pups to take his father's place. Rin Tin Tin Jr. starred in many more films. He would one day have a pup — named, of course, Rin Tin Tin III — who would help promote the use of military working dogs during World War II.

*Rin Tin Tin IV, great grandson of the original Rinty,
was also a star of the screen — in this case, television.
Here he is in 1956 with (from left to right) Lee Aaker,
James Brown, and Joe Sawyer, his co-stars on TV's*
The Adventures of Rin Tin Tin.

CHAPTER THREE

STUBBY

Rin Tin Tin only became famous after the war. The most celebrated American dog to actually serve in World War I was a bull terrier named Stubby. He had been smuggled overseas by the members of the first full outfit of the American Expeditionary Forces to land on French soil. Within two months of arriving, Stubby had made quite a name for himself. His actions, in fact, probably saved American lives — and forever changed the relationship between dog and soldier in the U.S. military.

Sweltering in their brown uniforms, the soldiers conducted drill after drill on the steamy athletic field at Yale University. It was the summer of 1917, and soon they would leave Connecticut to go overseas to fight in what was being called the Great War. A stocky bridle-and-white bull terrier padded around the training facility with his pink tongue lolling out the side of his mouth. He darted in and out of the company of soldiers.

Twenty-five-year-old Bob Conroy of the United States Army whistled to him. Conroy patted the dog on the head and gave him a bowlful of water. The muscular little guy at his feet wagged his stub of a tail in appreciation. He was given the name Stubby and, perhaps right then and there, the lost dog decided to adopt the tall kindly soldier.

Stubby quickly learned his new name and began basic training along with the enlisted men of the 26th Division of the 102nd Infantry Regiment, nicknamed the "Yankee Division." He slept with the soldiers through the night and awoke every morning to the sound of the bugle. He stepped in line and marched to the beat of the band.

Conroy taught the four-footed soldier how to salute. At the command, "Attention! Present arms," Stubby sat down on his haunches, raised his right paw to the side of his face, and stared into the eyes of the soldier until the salute was returned. When the bugle sounded for the call to eat, Stubby dashed to the mess tent, first in line. When he wasn't chasing down his next meal, the dog followed Conroy everywhere. By the time the leaves fell from the trees and the air cooled, dog and soldier were inseparable.

In mid-September, after three months of training, the soldiers loaded all of their belongings into trucks and horse-drawn wagons. Conroy patted Stubby on the head, sad at the thought of leaving him behind. Stubby did not take his eyes off Conroy, and he closely shadowed his favorite soldier for the rest of the day. "Stubby was sadly told it was useless to go any farther because dogs would not be permitted to board the ship," Conroy recalled. "Stubby naturally could not understand that."[1]

When the soldiers boarded the troop train for the seaport of Newport News, Virginia, Stubby followed Conroy into the darkened railroad car. Once in Newport News, the troops embarked on the *USS Minnesota,* a battleship headed for Europe. Conroy didn't want to break any rules, but how could he leave his best friend behind? By the time they left for France, Conroy had found a dog-loving accomplice in a crew member of the ship. The seaman walked the narrow gangplank with Stubby securely hidden in a blanket held under his arm.

Once aboard, he hid the dog in a coal bin in the engine room in the lower part of the *Minnesota.* When they finally were out to sea, Conroy removed Stubby from the coal bin and let him roam the ship.

American soldiers had begun wearing military identification tags around their necks to make it easier to identify them in case of death or injury. A pair of metal discs, they were known as "dog tags," and someone decided Stubby should have them, too. They hung from his leather collar and read:

STUBBY 102ND INF 26TH DIV[2]

Stormy skies and choppy waters plagued the long journey across the Atlantic Ocean. The angry seas tossed the massive ship, and many soldiers and livestock grew ill, but Stubby showed his worth as a soldier by never getting sick. Weeks later, the weary soldiers rejoiced at the sight of land as they finally reached the coast of France.

When the soldiers of Yankee Division got off the ship and made their way to base camp, the commanding officer noticed Stubby marching among the troops. While he pondered how to handle the situation, Stubby sat on his haunches and saluted. The trick must have softened the officer's heart, because he made Stubby the official mascot of the Yankee Division. In January of 1918, Col. John Henry "Machine Gun" Parker became the commanding officer of Conroy's regiment. Stubby somehow won his heart also. "Stubby was the only member of his regiment that could talk back to him and get away with it," his master said.[3]

At base camp, Conroy worked in the intelligence section, managing military information. He also stood guard, and when he did Stubby stood with him. Stubby jogged alongside his horse as he delivered important messages from headquarters.

The mascot dog had other jobs at the camp. If the soldiers were sick or sad, he came alongside and cheered them up. And when rats as large as cats infested the area, crawling over sleeping soldiers and feasting on the trash, Stubby hunted and killed the uninvited guests, as any good terrier would.

It was February 5, 1918, at Chemin des Dames, the northeast section of France, that Stubby saw his first action. After many weeks of hard training, the Yankee Division proceeded to the front line with orders to hold back the German advance and prevent them from capturing Paris. For over a month, Stubby and his soldier friends were under fire night and day. "During combat he seemed to know that no one could bother with him, and that he had to stay quietly under cover if he expected to remain a live mascot," Conroy recalled.[4]

The soldiers dug trenches and bunkers to keep them hidden and protected from machine gun and artillery fire.

World War I Trenches

The trenches had to be a particularly nasty place for dogs with their keen sense of smell. Sometimes soldiers needed to stay behind the protection of the trenches for months at a time and went without showers or the use of a bathroom. (The first gas masks were simply a scarf soaked in urine that covered the nose and mouth and counteracted the deadly fumes.) Mud from the rainy seasons caused fungal infections and the soldiers suffered from a disease called trench foot that could become so severe that the foot had to be amputated. The soldiers kept jam jars of glow worms in order to read maps and letters from loved ones in the gloomy dark of the trenches. Some days, soldiers in the trenches found themselves dodging gunfire, but other days were passed idly, waiting on the next full assault. To pass the time soldiers made "trench art," tiny figurines carved from wood, bones, and bullet casings.

A French courier dog leaps across a trench in World War I.
Dogs as well as pigeons were used to transmit messages where
telegraph wire could not be strung.

Stubby followed the actions of the men and learned to hide in the dugouts when bomb shells fell close.

Before long Stubby was diving for cover before the soldiers did. They guessed that Stubby could hear the whine of the shells before they could. Soon the troops learned to follow the dog's lead.

When the enemy attacked with mustard gas, air horns sounded a warning and the soldiers reached for their masks. The poisonous gas caused rashes, vomiting, blindness, and burning lungs. At times the yellow-green cloud of gas disfigured or disabled soldiers, and other times it meant certain death. One nurse, Vera Brittain, wrote: "I wish those people who talk about going on with this war whatever it costs could see the soldiers suffering from mustard gas poisoning. Great mustard-colored blisters, blind eyes, all sticky and stuck together, always fighting for breath, with voices a mere whisper, saying that their throats are closing and they know they will choke."[5]

One of the soldiers made a gas mask for the dog, but it didn't quite fit over his boxy nose. Stubby endured his first "battle wound" when a whiff of the gas made him physically ill. Once he understood the perils of the gas, Stubby alarmed the soldiers *before* the horns went off and quickly found the nearest sleeping bag in which to bury his nose. Mustard gas is lethal at doses of 60 parts per billion. A dog's nose is so sensitive, however, that it can pick up scents in traces as small as 500 parts per *trillion*.[6]

On the battlefield Stubby watched his fellow soldiers. He located wounded comrades as bullets whizzed over his head. He would either alert others to the injured man or else lay beside him, offering comfort until help arrived. Stubby roamed freely at all times. Some days he got lost and didn't return for a while, prompting the soldiers to joke that Stubby had gone AWOL, or "absent without leave."

One day while the dog was on patrol, he got a whiff of the familiar smell that had made him sick. He let out a loud bark and raced for the nearest trench. There he found a soldier passed out without a gas mask on. Stubby barked and barked. He tugged on the soldier's uniform. Nothing woke him. Warning horns sounded. Stubby barked frantically. He grabbed the soldier's coat sleeve and began pulling. Finally, Sgt. John J. Curtin opened his eyes and reached for his mask. Once the soldier's head cleared, he put a mask on Stubby. He hugged the dog and thanked him for saving his life. Later, the soldier wrote a poem about his hero:

He always knew when to duck the shells
And buried his nose at the first gas smells

After six weeks of constant fighting, Conroy received a promotion to Private First Class. Following a short break, the Yankee Division reported for duty on the northeastern front near Toul.

In the next battle, Stubby's luck ran out. A hand grenade exploded near him, spraying shrapnel everywhere. A piece of metal sliced through the dog's chest and left foreleg. Stubby howled. Conroy cradled Stubby in his arms and rushed him to the nearest first aid station.

The doctor recommended that the dog be taken to the Red Cross hospital for treatment. Conroy carried his fallen comrade to an ambulance filled with other wounded soldiers, then watched helplessly as the ambulance sped away through the dark night.

When Stubby arrived at the field hospital, an army surgeon removed the shrapnel embedded in the dog and stitched his wounds. He spent weeks recovering, and as he grew stronger he spent his days visiting the beds of wounded soldiers at the hospital, cheering up the sick and injured. Meanwhile his comrades back at Yankee Division sorely missed their mascot. Six weeks later he was released to join the troops again. Stubby, said Conroy, "was like the proverbial cat; he seemed to have many lives."[7]

In August of 1918, the Yankee Division liberated the French town of Chateau-Thierry. After hearing the stories of the dog's wartime heroism, the women of the town crafted a coat of honor for Stubby. They sewed STUBBY, 102ND U.S. INFANTRY onto the light brown jacket made from soft chamois leather. A wreath of Allied countries' flags and service patches from the Yankee Division adorned the coat.

Wearing his brand new coat, Stubby set out with Conroy for Paris on a ten-day leave. Their official travel documents contained both their names. Near the Arc de Triomphe, two sisters stopped to see the stylish soldier dog. They petted and fussed over Stubby. As the girls said their goodbyes, Stubby nudged the younger one, demanding more attention. The girls lingered a little longer — and as they did, a runaway horse and buggy flew by on the street they were planning to enter moments earlier. After that incident, Stubby's legend only grew. He not only saved the lives of soldiers, but most likely the lives of two Parisian girls as well.

One night, while the soldiers slept in their muddy dug-outs, Stubby heard the sound of bushes rustling and went to investigate. A soldier he didn't recognize emerged from the bushes. The soldier tried befriending the dog, but Stubby was having none of it. The soldier turned to run, and the dog charged at full speed, leaping and grabbing the fleeing soldier by the seat of his pants. The screams from Stubby's hostage alerted the sleeping troops. The enemy soldier was arrested. For his actions, Stubby earned medals and emblems for his new jacket and the soldiers named him honorary sergeant.

On November 2, 1918, Conroy and Stubby were wounded in action by a mustard gas attack. Only nine days later, on November 11, the war came to an end.

President Woodrow Wilson sailed to Europe to sign a peace treaty. On Christmas Day, the President of the United States requested to meet Sergeant Stubby, the famous

Gen. John Pershing, commander of the Allied Expeditionary Forces in World War I, inspects Stubby as Bob Conroy (left) looks on proudly.

four-footed soldier. The dog saluted President Wilson, and then he stuck his paw out so they could "shake hands."

In March 1919 Stubby returned home to America with Conroy. This time, instead of being smuggled onto the ship, the mascot of the 102nd U.S. Infantry trotted aboard the *Agamemnon* at his partner's side. Conroy, who by war's end had been promoted to corporal, had kept a large leather-bound scrapbook filled with photos and memories of his service, including seventeen battles on the western front, alongside his best friend.

Stubby traveled the nation to veterans' commemorations and performed in vaudeville shows. He earned $62.50 for three days' work doing theatrical appearances, more than twice the weekly salary of the average American.[9] He was made an honorary member of the American Red Cross and the American Legion. The YMCA issued Stubby a lifetime membership card good for "three bones a day and a place to sleep."[8] He met three sitting presidents.

In 1921 Corporal Conroy brought his famous war dog along when he moved to Washington, D.C., to attend law school in Georgetown. Stubby became mascot to the football team. Halfway through one game, wearing a blue and gray cape with the letter G on the sides, Stubby nudged a football around the field to the delight of the crowd. Some credit this with the start of the halftime show. The Georgetown University mascot is a bulldog, thanks to this soldier dog.[9]

Stubby's military accomplishments did not go unnoticed. Gen. John Pershing, who commanded the American Expeditionary Forces during the war, presented him with a gold medal made by the Humane Society and declared him to be a "hero of the highest caliber."[10] The bravery and loyalty with which he served made a statement that dogs were an asset on the battlefield. Stubby's starred military career helped inspire the creation of the 'K-9 Corps' in World War II.

Bob Conroy and Stubby, both in uniform and wearing the medals each of them earned in World War I.

CHAPTER FOUR

SMOKY

For twenty years the world lived under an uneasy truce. In 1933, Adolf Hitler came to power in Germany and began a massive arms buildup. When World War II (1939-1945) broke out, Hitler already had 200,000 trained war dogs. Japan had 75,000 dogs ready for action. Would America finally raise up a canine corps?

The answer came just days after the bombing of Pearl Harbor and the entry of the U.S. into the war in 1941. A nationally known dog breeder, Alene Erlanger, approached the leadership of the Army with strong words of advice. "The dog world must play a part in this thing," she declared. "Other countries have used dogs for years and ours has not. They've got to do it!"[1]

Soon after, Secretary of War Henry Stimson ordered every branch of the United States military to train dogs for search and rescue, as sentry (guard) dogs, and for detection and scouting.

Besides purchasing dogs, the military asked American citizens to donate their pets in a program called Dogs for

Defense. In January 1942 American Kennel Club director Harry I. Caesar contacted dog trainers and clubs across the country to ask for their help. Thousands of families felt it their patriotic duty to send the family dog off to war. After the dogs left the country, their owners sent letters and treats to the war zone to keep connected with their beloved pets.

Dogs could be male or female but had to be one to five years of age, at least twenty-five inches high, and weigh a minimum of fifty pounds. After passing a physical examination, each dog was tested to make sure that he or she was not gun-shy or timid. The breed of the dog was considered secondary to the general competence of the dog. The military accepted suitable breeds as wide ranging

The military promoted the Dogs for Defense program
heavily during World War II. Thousands of American
families donated their pets to the military.

as Dalmatians, boxers, collies, German shepherds, and Doberman pinschers.

So when a Yorkshire terrier appeared in a war zone in New Guinea, an island off the coast of Australia, it left everyone scratching their heads. The dog weighed about four pounds and stood only seven inches tall. Surely this little pooch had not been sent to fight the war.

***

It was March of 1944. Aerial photographer Ed Downey's jeep had quit running, leaving him along a primitive road in the New Guinean countryside. As he looked under the hood, a strange whining sound came from the jungle. Downey went to investigate the noise. To his surprise a tiny blonde head bopped up and down inside of a foxhole — a man-made hole used to hide or seek shelter from an enemy or gunfire. A little dog was frantically clawing at the dirt, desperate to escape.

Downey was not fond of dogs, but he figured someone in his unit might like a companion. Back at base camp, he gave the dog to a sergeant, who named her Smokums, gave her a haircut, and secured her to a tire inside the motor pool tent.

When photographer Bill Wynne walked in, he bumped into Smokums. He bent down and looked into a pair of almond-shaped eyes above a black button nose. He had never seen a dog breed so petite and lovely. The dog licked his hand with its tiny tongue. *What kind of beast is this?* Wynne thought. *It's a dizzy little poodle!*

Wynne instantly asked to buy Smokums, who was in fact a Yorkshire terrier. He offered two pounds Australian money, or $6.44 in U.S. currency at the time.

"Make it three and she's yours," the sergeant said.

Wynne took a second look at the dog with the bad haircut, wondered about her health, and decided to hang onto his money. He admired her spirit and the twinkle in her eyes — but just the thought of getting attached to the animal only to lose her to malnutrition, pythons in the jungles, or the horrors of the war was more than he thought he could bear. But Wynne, like Rin Tin Tin's owner, Lee Duncan, had lived in an orphanage and knew what it meant to be abandoned. He said a prayer for the little pooch.

The next day the sergeant walked into the photo lab.

"Hey, Wynne," he said, "want to buy the dog for two pounds? I want to get back in a poker game tonight."[2]

Wynne didn't hesitate to hand over the money. He changed her name to Smoky and looked around for something to feed her. The soldiers lived on an unappetizing diet of coffee, dehydrated potatoes, powdered milk, eggs, mutton, canned fruit, and something called "bully beef," which was like corned beef hash. Wynne opened up a tin of bully beef and Smoky quickly gobbled it up.

From that moment on they were inseparable. Every morning Wynne would wash and shave himself, using his helmet as a sink. Then he would fill the helmet with fresh water and give Smoky a bath.

After that, it was time for her daily training. Wynne started out with simple commands: sit, stay, heel. She quickly mastered those, so he moved on to more complicated tricks.

"Dead dog" became one of her favorites. Wynne pointed his finger at her and shouted, "Bang!" Smoky fell down and lay very still on her side. Wynne poked and prodded the little dog, but she never moved a muscle. Even when he picked her up and rolled her from hand to hand, Smoky would hang limply from his palm. Finally Wynne would set Smoky down and walk away. He would wait a moment before quietly giving the command: "Okay." With that Smoky would spring to life and run happily to her soldier.

An American military magazine called *Yank Down Under,* popular with many of the Australian and American troops, held a contest in search of the best mascot in the South Pacific area. The competition included all kinds of creatures, including monkeys and parrots.

As a photographer, Wynne could think of a number of creative ways to feature his petite princess. He took a photo of Smoky sitting in his helmet to emphasize her tiny stature. He cut up some parachute material to customize a Smoky-sized chute. One of his buddies took the dog up to the top of a tree as Wynne positioned himself below. The soldier let Smoky drop, and she sailed through the air in her parachute as Wynne's camera fired away. After landing in an outstretched blanket held by other soldiers, everyone cheered. Smoky, not sure what to make of all this, just wagged her tail.

By this time, the little dog had won over most of the base with her talent show, a series of complicated tricks performed to music. She also amused them with her antics of chasing wild hump-backed guinea hens and exotic butterflies.

One evening Wynne's baseball team was playing a game and a soldier offered to hold the dog to keep her off the field. But once the first hitter made contact with the ball, Smoky shot like a missile from the soldier's hands. Just as the third baseman went to scoop up the ball, the dog clamped her mouth around it. The force of the ball knocked her straight into the mitt of the fielder, who fortunately did not try to throw the ball — and the dog attached to it — across the field.

One morning Wynne had to leave Smoky behind when he developed a high fever. On his third day in the hospital, his comrades decided to cheer him up by smuggling Smoky

Army photographer Bill Wynne bathed Smoky in his helmet — and took this picture of her inside it to feature her petite size.

in for a visit. They also brought a large manila envelope that had arrived in the mail for him. Wynne opened the envelope. It contained several copies of *Yank Down Under* along with a letter announcing that Smoky had won the mascot contest. He smiled broadly and said, "This is the best medicine a guy can get."[3]

The nurses at the hospital discovered the little dog in Wynne's room and fell for her. "Can we take her on our rounds?" one nurse asked. "The guys will love her. She's one of them!" At bedside after bedside, Smoky — presented as "the Champion Mascot of the South Pacific Area" — cheered up the battle-weary troops, giving a morale boost to the sick and wounded.

The commanding officer at the army hospital where Bill recuperated was Dr. Charles Mayo of Mayo Clinic fame. Observing how Smoky had lifted spirits, Dr. Mayo granted permission for the dog to live at the hospital for Wynne's five-day stay. She returned every evening to Wynne's cot, tired but well-fed, and snuggled by her soldier.

After their release, Wynne and Smoky visited soldiers at hospitals whenever time allowed.[4] Smoky is widely regarded as the world's first therapy dog.

Back at the base, the dog team continued to entertain the troops, with Smoky performing her numerous tricks to music. When the air raid sirens blew, the music stopped and Wynne would grab his Yorkie and cover her while he huddled in the bomb shelter. They survived 150 air raids while stationed in New Guinea.

On combat missions, the corporal was expected to fly along and take pictures. Smoky made it clear that she did not want to be left behind. Wynne figured, why not? "I felt our chances of survival were good," he recalled. Besides, "a mascot brings good luck to the team."

The duo flew a dozen combat missions together, and Wynne shared eight battle awards with her. The closest call the pair had during the war wasn't on land or in the air, but at sea.

While on board a landing ship tank off the coast of Mindoro, an island in the Philippines, Wynne and a few others were playing cards. Suddenly the ship's alarms blared, warning of an imminent attack. Fourteen planes piloted by Japanese fighters appeared in the sky, on a *kamikaze* (suicide) mission — prepared to crash into ships, killing others as they died.

The artillery fired upon the planes, which fell short of the ships and splashed into the water, creating giant geysers. Suddenly, a huge yellow flash lit up the sky just a few feet from the ship. Smoky trembled and pulled on her leash. Wynne took her to another part of the ship where the Jeeps were parked. Using the vehicles for cover, they crouched down and Wynne covered the Yorkie's delicate ears with his hands as the deck bounced and vibrated.

Finally, the all-clear signal sounded. When Wynne stood up, he realized all of the men who remained standing had injuries, some severe. Had he stayed where he was instead of covering his trembling partner and hitting the deck, he likely would have taken shrapnel from U.S. machine guns.

"From that day on," he said, "I had the belief that Smoky was my angel."[5]

Therapy Dogs and Service Dogs

Although dogs have long brought comfort to the sick and wounded, the widespread use of therapy dogs began in the 1970s when a nurse named Elaine Smith founded Therapy Dogs International. The organization has registered over 20,000 dog teams and regularly evaluates every dog for good temperament. A therapy dog must be able to sit patiently with people of different ages and behaviors. Science has proven that therapy dogs lower blood pressure, reduce stress, and ward off depression in the people they serve.

A service dog, however, is trained to assist just one person and is assigned to that individual at all times. People request service dogs to help cope with a specific disabling problem, such as a physical handicap or emotional disorder. Therapy dogs bring comfort to the sick or infirm. Service dogs help individuals live their lives — including veterans suffering the effects of post-traumatic stress brought on by combat.

Whatever the job they have to do, service and therapy dogs offer people the healing benefits of unconditional love.[6]

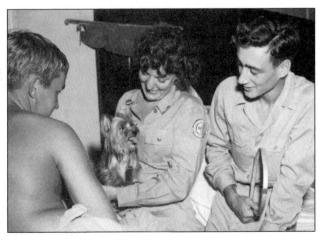

Smoky visits a base hospital in her role as a therapy dog.

She served as a tireless and uncomplaining worker. At an air base in the Philippines, Wynne was asked if Smoky could be coaxed to pull communications lines under an airstrip. A message had been delivered to the commanding officers warning of Japanese paratroopers invading nearby areas with sneak attacks, killing soldiers and destroying aircraft. About forty fighter planes, sitting wing tip to wing tip, were on the steel matting of the runway. With no communication lines set up, the soldiers and their equipment were at high risk.

Smoky would have to travel seventy feet through a narrow drainage pipe, pulling a string attached to her collar. If she succeeded, she would save the men about three days' work in a treacherous area where they would be constantly exposed to enemy fire.

Wynne agreed to let Smoky give it a try. Smoky disappeared into one end of the pipe, only eight inches in diameter. At the other end Wynne coaxed her along: "Come, Smoky, come."

After a while, he could see the outline of his tiny dog against the light.

"You can do it, Smoky," he said.

Suddenly he spotted two amber eyes peering through the dust about fifteen feet away. "She's here!" he shouted to the others.

Smoky broke into a run and flew into Wynne's outstretched arms.[7]

News of Smoky's big day spread through the camp. A four-pound Yorkie did the job of seventy men, and got it done in about three minutes. In that same amount of time

*After World War II, Smoky and Bill Wynne performed
on local TV shows in Cleveland, Ohio.*

Smoky went from being a war dog mascot to a war dog
hero. Thanks to her exploits, she and Wynne came home
after the war in November 1945 to great fanfare. A front-
page story of the *Cleveland Press* had pictures of her under
the headline:

TINY WAR DOG HOME WITH BAG OF TRICKS
LEARNED IN 2 YEARS OF PACIFIC SERVICE

Fan mail poured in. When televisions came to the Cleveland area, Wynne and Smoky were offered a spot on a children's show, "Mr. Pokie and his Dog Smoky." In the 42 weeks that the show aired, Smoky never did the same trick twice. Later, the duo appeared in their own Sunday-morning show, "How to Train Your Dog with Bill Wynne and Smoky."

The dog team continued to visit hospitals, nursing homes, and orphanages until Smoky's death on February 21, 1957. Grace Guderian, a nurse working at the local Veterans Administration hospital, read the dog's obituary in the *Cleveland Plain Dealer* and called Wynne with some startling news.

Guderian had been an Army lieutenant during the war, assigned to a field hospital in Australia. On December 25, 1943, she received a Yorkshire terrier puppy from her fiancé, which given the date she decided to name Christmas. Lt. Guderian took along her new puppy when she was transferred to New Guinea — where the dog went missing. The mystery of the Yorkie in the foxhole seemed finally to be solved.

Whether called Christmas or Smoky, she was a little dog that went on to do big things.

Top: Page One of the Cleveland Press, *December 7, 1945.*
Bottom: Ladies from the Red Cross made Smoky a corporal's jacket on
which medals of honor and awards for bravery were sewn, including
two presidential unit citations and the Good Conduct Ribbon.

CHAPTER FIVE

SHOULD A DOG GET A SILVER STAR?

World War II presented many hardships for American soldiers. If they were lucky, there was a dog nearby for emotional support, as it was for the men who shared their lives with Smoky, Stubby, and Dog Jack. Sometimes these mascot dogs would surprise their soldiers by performing life-saving tasks, as Smoky did when she ran communications lines through a dangerous airfield.

For the first time, the U.S. military in World War II trained and deployed working dogs into combat. Each branch set up several platoons especially for dogs, though the troops and news media usually just referred to them as "the K-9 Corps." They were valuable both as scout dogs and patrol dogs.

As scouts, dogs constantly alerted to the presence of potential threats beyond the hearing or sight range of their soldiers. After Allied forces captured enemy territory, dog teams went out on patrol to sniff out land mines planted by retreating forces, as well as search nearby caves for hiding enemy combatants.

A picture of Chips from the war scrapbook of Sgt. Herson L. Whitley, who served in the Army's Third Infantry Division.

After the U.S. captured the Pacific island of Guam in 1944, the Marine Corps sent in two platoons of canines, mostly Doberman pinschers, to clear the island of mines and Japanese snipers hiding in caves. On one patrol, a Doberman named Kurt alerted his handler to Japanese forces just ahead, waiting in ambush. Kurt's silent warning saved the lives of 250 Marines from the mortar attack that followed. When asked where to bury Kurt, the first canine killed in action on the island, Capt. William Putney's commanding officer told him, "Bury him with the men. He's a marine just like the rest of them."[1]

Guam proved to be a dangerous place. Forty-five of the sixty dogs in the platoons were killed or wounded by explosives and sniper fire. Numerous war memorials have been built in tribute to the service of dogs in World War II, including the Dobermans who gave their lives in Guam.

Some in the military wanted to go further than merely praising the owners of outstanding working dogs. They wanted to bestow military honors on the dogs themselves. That led to controversy and a new policy that exists to this day.

You could say the trouble started one morning in 1942 when a dog in Pleasantville, New York, attacked the garbage man. The dog was Chips, a Husky-collie-shepherd mix belonging to Edward Wren and his family. Mr. Wren had gotten fed up with his unruly dog, and decided a visit to boot camp might be in order. So Chips was "volunteered" to the Dogs for Defense program.

He trained as a sentry dog, and proved to be a model student. The Army chose him for elite duty with the Third Infantry Division. Chips arrived in Africa in January 1943, just in time to stand guard outside the historic meeting between President Franklin D. Roosevelt and British prime minister Winston Churchill in Casablanca, Morocco.

Later that year, the Third Infantry took part in the invasion of the island of Sicily, a campaign known as Operation Husky. During one especially intense day of fighting, Chips broke away before his handler knew what was happening. He dashed directly toward a enemy nest a few hundred yards away. Taking on machine-gun fire, Chips jumped inside the nest and sank his teeth into the first man he saw. Chips suffered battle wounds, but all four enemy combatants were captured.

The Husky mix became the toast of Operation Husky. News accounts hailed his daring dash. Chips received a personal visit from the commander of the Allied forces

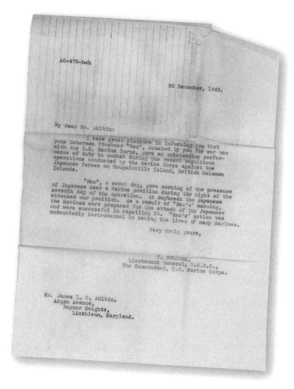

Dogs saved countless lives in World War II. In this letter dated December 20, 1943, the commandant of the Marine Corps informs the owner of Rex, a Doberman pinscher donated to the military, that the dog was on patrol in the British Solomon Islands when he alerted Marines to the presence of approaching enemy soldiers. "Rex's action was undoubtedly instrumental in saving the lives of many Marines," the letter reads.

himself, Gen. Dwight D. Eisenhower. When Eisenhower bent down to pet the dog, Chips did what he had been trained to do when strangers came too close — he bit the general.[2]

In November 1943, the Army decided to award Chips two of its highest military honors. He received the Purple Heart, the medal given out since the Revolutionary War to soldiers killed or wounded in combat. (Stubby had been the first dog awarded a Purple Heart, for his wounds from the World War I gas attack.) Chips was also awarded the Silver Star Medal, given for "gallantry in action against an enemy of the United States." Two months later, Chips received the Distinguished Service Cross for "extraordinary heroism." Only the Medal of Honor, the nation's highest military award, is more prestigious.[3]

Then the humans began to bark. The commander of the Purple Heart Foundation complained to President Roosevelt, saying that awards for soldiers should not go to animals. Others, including members of Congress, also criticized the decision to bestow such high honors upon a dog. Finally Army Maj. Gen. James A. Ulio ruled that Chips had earned his medals and could keep them. In the future, however, no dog would be eligible for military honors that are given out to humans.[4]

That ruling has stood for more than 70 years. Should it? Section 578.10 of the Code of Federal Regulations states that the Distinguished Service Cross should only be awarded for "acts of heroism [that] must have been so notable and have involved risk of life so extraordinary as to set the individual apart from his comrades." No one doubts that what Chips did went above and beyond the call of duty — after all, his duty was to stand guard, not attack the enemy. But was he really aware of the "extraordinary" danger he was in?

On the other hand, some argue that military dogs have saved tens of thousands of lives over the years. Heroic deeds matter, whether the hero knows it or not. Men and women who receive military honors for bravery often say that they do not consider their acts of valor to be heroic or extraordinary. They say they were just doing their duty.

In recent years, dog advocates have been urging the military to create a special award for members of the canine corps. They point to Great Britain, which in 1943 began awarding the Dickin Medal for gallantry by animals. Over the years the British have honored thirty-one dogs, thirty-five messenger pigeons, five horses, and a cat.

In April 2016 a German shepherd mix named Lucca was honored with a Dickin Medal. But Lucca wasn't a British military dog. She conducted more than four hundred patrols during six years of service for the *United States*. She is the first U.S. Marine Corps dog to receive this honor.

On her final patrol in 2012, a street bomb blew up underneath Lucca. Her handler, Cpl. Juan Rodriguez, carried her to safety and applied a tourniquet to her injured leg, which was later amputated.

"I stayed with her constantly throughout her operation and her recovery," Cpl. Rodriguez said. "She had saved my life on so many occasions. I had to make sure that I was there for her when she needed me."[5]

Lucca and her handler, Cpl. Juan M. Rodriguez. During her military service, Lucca uncovered more than forty improvised explosive devices.

CHAPTER SIX

ROGER WILCO

Throughout the summer of 1943 the 385th Bombardment Group had been flying missions over Germany, dropping bombs on the factories where Hitler built his war machine. Based out of England, they flew B-17 bombers, huge "Flying Fortresses" that could take a beating from the enemy and still make it back to base.

Every B-17 had a name. One was called *Sack Time*. The crew named it as a tribute to the little dog who slept curled up in a blanket in the nose of the plane during every training mission.

Lt. Leslie Reichardt, a member of the 385th Bomb Group's 549th Squadron, was on a three-day leave that summer when he saw a jet-black cocker spaniel for sale at a pet shop. Reichardt, who had a dog back home in Ohio named Toots, was longing for a canine companion, so he purchased the dog and brought him back to the air base. The spaniel instantly won over the boys of the 549th, and they gave their new mascot a name — Roger Wilco, aircraft talk for "yes, will comply."

On the evening of August 17, 1943, Roger was at the base with radio operator Egbert Rude, who was writing in his diary.

"Our bunkhouse rather deserted tonight," he began. "My crew is out on a three-day mission. I was grounded due to a bad head cold — the first flight I have missed.... Roger, our little spaniel, is sick. I have just returned from the veterinarian with him — will have some doctoring until our crew gets back."

Sgt. Rude was glad to have Roger with him sharing this lonely night in England. He did not know it yet, but they would spend many nights comforting each other.

***

Two days earlier, the B-17 carrying Lt. Reichardt and nine others had been shot down over Dunkirk, Germany.

By September 6, Sgt. Rude had learned about his comrades' fate. But he also had some good news to report to his diary: "Ten chutes were seen to come out of our ship, so I expect to see all of my gang again someday."

He added, "Roger is much improved — but needs a bath."[1]

The crew of the *Sack Time* had parachuted to safety and into the hands of the Nazis, who made them prisoners of war. That made Sgt. Rude the sole guardian of their mascot dog.

He started writing letters to Lt. Reichardt's family, giving them updates on Roger. When he received his orders to return to the United States, he let the family know he would be bringing the cocker spaniel with him. The

*Above: A photographer in a nearby plane captures the moment when
Sack Time (circled), carrying pilot Leslie Reichardt and
nine crew members, is shot down over enemy territory in Germany.
All ten men parachuted to safety and were taken prisoner.
Below: Roger Wilco and the crew of Sack Time.*

Reichardts looked forward to caring for Roger until their POW came home.

Rude sailed from England aboard the *Queen Mary*. There were rules on the big ship, and one of them was "no dogs allowed." But the sergeant thought of another rule from the military — *no soldier left behind*. He stashed Roger in his duffel bag and walked on board. After the dog was discovered, Rude was ordered to the mess hall. His punishment was "K.P.," or kitchen patrol, peeling potatoes for the rest of the journey.

Soon Roger Wilco joined his new family in the United States. Letters arrived from Lt. Reichardt, who was being held in a prisoner of war camp. "Is Roger home yet?" he wrote his wife on June 17, 1944. "How is he? Suppose he will remember me? Bet he has grown!"

On June 19, after receiving sad news about his other dog, he wrote his parents, "Sorry to hear about Toots, but I guess it was for the best. You will probably get Roger by now for company.... Hope I get a snapshot of him soon."[2]

***

One month after Germany surrendered, Leslie Reichardt stepped off a train in Marion, Ohio, a free man. His wife Betty, his mother Beryl, and his father Arliss greeted the soldier — and so did his dog, who was straining at the leash, wagging his stubby tail. Roger pulled free of the leash and charged Reichardt, anxious to get his paws on him.

The lieutenant had suffered hardships in POW camp, and he was not well. While he recuperated in bed, Roger made himself a sentry dog. If a visitor tried to enter Reichardt's bedroom, Roger stopped them with a warning growl. Only when the lieutenant was seated and ready for guests did the dog step aside. Even then, he kept a wary eye on the caller. He lay at the soldier's feet until the visit ended, then went back to guarding the entrance.

Roger Wilco never let Lt. Reichardt out of his sight again.

Leslie Reichardt and Roger Wilco, after the war.

CHAPTER SEVEN

NEMO

After World War II, most of the military's dog platoons were disbanded and the pets were returned to their owners. The military had classified the dogs as equipment and could have disposed of them, but the United States spent time and money to retrain the surviving dogs for their return to domestic life, out of respect for their service to the country and for the citizens who donated their family dogs. Letters were written thanking the government for taking such good care of their pets and for training them so well.

Dogs were not needed on the battlefield again until the Korean War (1950-1953). At that time only one active dog platoon remained — the 26th Scout Dog Platoon out of Fort Riley, Kansas. The dogs and their handlers arrived in Korea in early 1952 to become the eyes and the ears of the soldiers in one of the most vulnerable areas of the country. One year later, their success was recorded in General Orders 114: "The unbroken record of faithful and gallant performance of these missions by the individual handlers and their dogs in support of the patrols have saved countless casualties through giving early warning to the friendly patrol of threats to its security."[1]

After the Korean War, President Eisenhower ordered the military budget cut to peacetime levels. That meant the end to many programs, including the training of war dogs. Rumors spread that the government was not only going to close the training facilities but also euthanize — kill — all the dogs.

Letters of outrage poured into the Department of Defense. "There isn't a thing on this old Mother Earth that is so faithful, so loyal, so willing to give his life for his master than a dog," wrote Wendy Bogue of Eau Claire, Wisconsin. "Disposing of these dogs would be the greatest mistake the Army could make."[2] Veterans wrote letters, sharing story after story of how the dogs saved their lives and the lives of many others. The Department of Defense, however, merely deactivated the war dog program in 1957.

The following year, 1958, a new facility known today as the Military Working Dog School was created at Lackland Air Force Base in San Antonio, Texas. The Lackland school was established to train better military working dog teams. Within a few years it would be sending them to South Vietnam, a place few Americans could find on a map.

Approximately 4,900 dogs and 10,000 dog handlers served the U.S. in the Vietnam War (1964-1975). These dogs worked as sentries, scouts, and mine detectors in all four branches of the military, but mostly the Army. Sentry dogs were assigned to the outer limits of U.S. military bases, which were often surrounded by jungle. In such an environment it was difficult for humans to see an approaching enemy. But a dog could see, hear, and smell someone sneaking up on the base, and make a beeline for the intruder. This ability earned sentry dogs the name "guided muzzles" in Vietnam.

Others were trained as scout dogs. Scout dog teams walked "point," that is, in front of all of the troops. Walking point is sometimes called the "tip of the spear," and it is the most dangerous job in combat patrol because the leader is the first one the enemy will see or shoot. The lives of the men following the scout dog team counted on being alerted to danger before danger found them.

The dogs' highly refined senses alerted the humans to explosive land mines, snipers hidden in the bush, and stashes of hidden weapons. Scout dog teams discovered over 175 explosives in just the first five months of 1968.[3] From January 1968 to October 1969, scout dogs detected 1,181 snipers and captured 509 prisoners. Others went behind enemy lines to locate missing soldiers and pilots whose planes had been shot down. The Viet Cong realized the threat these dogs posed and made the canine corps a primary target for sniper fire.

For Vietnam, several breeds were tested including Bouvier des Flandres, giant schnauzers, German shepherds, Doberman pinschers, Rottweilers, and the Belgian Malinois. As a result of this testing, German shepherds became the preferred dog in Vietnam. They worked hard, even in cold and hot weather, performed the widest variety of tasks, and had as an impressive a bite as the Doberman pinscher. Labrador retrievers were also found to be useful because their highly-sensitive noses could detect weapons even in swamps and wetlands. That ability would be very useful in the jungles of Vietnam.

In all, military dogs were credited with saving the lives of over 10,000 American soldiers in Vietnam.[4] Most performed their tasks with little fanfare or attention from the outside world. And then there was Nemo.

Among the teams that departed Lackland for Vietnam in 1966 was a black and tan German shepherd named Nemo A534 — Nemo for short. He had finished a rigorous eight-week boot camp with flying colors, learning to run through

Nemo on sentry duty with his first handler,
Leonard Bryant, in Vietnam.

obstacle courses, detect land mines, and attack the enemy on command. (At Lackland, the enemy was played by a soldier wearing a bite-proof burlap suit, his face covered with a steel mask.)

Airman 2nd Class Leonard Bryant accompanied Nemo to Vietnam and delivered him to a new handler, Airman 2nd Class Robert Throneburg. They ran through obstacle courses and worked on obedience drills. The soldier praised the dog, positively reinforcing his efforts. Throneburg groomed Nemo. They ate, played, and wrestled together. At the end of a long day, the dog slept alongside the soldier. "You put your heart, soul, and trust in your dog when you are working in that environment," Throneburg said. "They are your best friend."[5]

Nemo and Throneburg were one of sixty teams deployed to guard the massive Tan Son Nhut Air Base near the South Vietnamese capital of Saigon. A large field, called a bomb dump, held stacks of crates containing explosives waiting to be loaded aboard the planes. Tan Son Nhut was one of the busiest airports in the world. Patrols rotated, guarding the area day and night. The enemy kept creeping closer, trying to destroy the aircraft, the ammunition, and the facilities.

In the early hours of December 4, 1966, a small detachment of Viet Cong, the North Vietnamese army, tunneled beneath the security fence and under fields of land mines. They stormed the base and had hoped to surprise the Americans, but a sentry dog unit near one of the runways picked up the Viet Cong's movements and alerted the troops. In the ensuing battle one soldier, George Bevich, and three sentry dogs named Toby, Cubby, and Rebel were killed in action, but the base was saved from major harm. With the bomb dump secured, planes resumed landing at the air base only eight hours later.

As the sun set the following evening, the dog teams of the 377th Air Police Squadron headed for their assignments. No one spoke a word as thoughts of their fallen comrades weighed heavily on their minds.

With orders to work the night shift guarding the perimeter, twenty-two-year-old Throneburg sat with his dog in the back of the K-9 transport truck. Of all the places they could have been assigned, Throneburg and Nemo had orders to patrol the eerie graveyard located near the runway, the same place where all the action happened the day before.

The truck stopped in front of the cemetery to let the dog handler and his partner out. Side by side they walked among the tombstones. Stars twinkled in the darkened skies. Six-foot blades of elephant grass surrounded the graveyard, adding to the spooky, closed-in feel.

As they passed a Vietnamese shrine, Nemo hesitated. His eyes shone in the darkness. His ears perked up. The fur between his shoulder blades rose along with his tail.

Throneburg recognized the signal that something lurked ahead. He whispered into his radio, informing the command center of Nemo's alert and their whereabouts. Then the soldier bent down close to the dog's ear and whispered, "Watch him!" Throneburg unclipped the leash. Nemo's muscles tightened like a coil. The dog leapt forward, unleashing incredible speed.

Nemo with Robert Throneburg and Leonard Bryant, his two handlers.

The hidden enemy opened fire. *Rat-tat-da-tat!* Throneburg stormed into the high grass, firing his weapon. The sound of gunshots filled the air. Two shots blasted Throneburg's left shoulder, knocking him to the ground. Nemo lunged at the shooter, and as he did, a bullet tore through his right eye and exited through his mouth.

Although badly wounded, Nemo, jaws snapping, attacked the Viet Cong soldier. Throneburg lay on the ground, firing his gun wildly. At long last, Nemo subdued the enemy soldier, who lay motionless a few feet away.

With the immediate threat eliminated, Throneburg passed out from excruciating pain. Wounded and blinded in his right eye, Nemo crawled back to Throneburg. The dog covered his partner with his body.

When the security police arrived, Throneburg lay unconscious, with 85-pound Nemo still draped over him — and not about to let anyone near his handler. Deep, guttural growls and clattering teeth met any attempt to remove the injured soldier from the battlefield. Fortunately, Nemo's first handler, Leonard Bryant, was still on base. He rushed to the scene and got Nemo to move away from Throneburg.

While a medical doctor operated on the wounded soldier, base veterinarian Capt. Raymond T. Huston operated on his partner. "When Nemo was brought to me he was in pretty bad shape," Dr. Huston said, "I had to do skin grafts on his face and perform a tracheotomy to help him breathe. "The dog's right eye had to be removed.[6]

News reporters, who were already at the airstrip covering the Viet Cong attack from the day before, soon got wind of Nemo's daring deed. Always on the lookout for a feel-good story in a war zone, they reported on the dog who saved the life of his handler and lost an eye.

American children sent cards and letters, like this boy in Seattle:

> *Dear Nemo,*
>
> *I am sending this letter because I love dogs and the last dog I had died at the age of four months. I hope you get well.*
>
> *Your Friend,*
> *Jeff White[7]*

Throneburg's injuries were too serious to be cared for at the base. He would have to travel to an air base in Japan for further treatment — which meant he would be separated from Nemo, possibly forever. While lying in the hospital awaiting his flight to Japan, he had a visit from Bryant and Nemo. The dog licked his face. To Throneburg, the dog's expression seemed to say: *Okay, here I am, boss.*[8]

It broke his heart to think that he would never see Nemo again. He wondered if his partner would be assigned to a new handler, or worse, that he would be euthanized because his injuries were too severe. He embraced Nemo one last time and thanked the dog for saving his life.

Throneburg recovered from his wounds and received a hero's welcome back in the U.S., along with three military honors: two Purple Hearts and the Bronze Star Medal. The Bronze Star came with a quarter-inch metal "V" on the ribbon. The V is for valor.[9]

As for Nemo, his injuries proved too serious for him to report back to duty. He was sent home to the United States — the first sentry dog retired from active service. At Lackland, Nemo was greeted by Captain Robert M. Sullivan, the officer in charge of sentry dog training.

"I have to keep from getting involved with individual dogs in this program," Sullivan said, "but I can't help feeling a little emotional about this dog. He shows how valuable a dog is to his handler in staying alive."[10]

Nemo would spend the rest of his life in private living quarters at Lackland, next to the veterinary facility. He toured the country with Capt. Sullivan, making television appearances and serving as the military working dog program's best recruiter.

Nemo died at age eleven on March 15, 1973. He is buried at Lackland. His gravestone reads, "Nemo A534," and a plaque tells of his heroism. It serves as a reminder to future students of the importance of a dog to his handler — and to all of the troops.

Looking back, Throneburg credits his faithful companion with helping the military working dog program to grow. "Capt. Sullivan and Nemo started a recruitment program and developed the war dog program that has evolved into what it is today," said Throneburg. "It makes me very proud."[11]

Nemo after the surgery in which his injured eye was removed.

Robert and Patricia Throneburg visit Nemo's memorial kennel at Lackland Air Force Base.

CHAPTER EIGHT

CLIPPER

If Nemo's story showed the military working dog program at its best, the story of Clipper demonstrated the military's treatment of its canine corps at its cold-hearted worst. The memory of Clipper still haunts one soldier who knew and loved him.

Within a year of the first deployments to Vietnam, military working dogs proved so effective at saving lives in the ground war that there were not enough dog teams to fill the demand. And so, just as happened in World War II, the call went out for families to send their pets to fight alongside the soldiers.

Clipper's family must have believed their German shepherd would make a good soldier, because they sent him from the comfort of his California home to attend war dog schools in Texas and Georgia. He passed a rigorous sixteen-week boot camp where he learned to navigate obstacle courses, crawl on command, respond to voice and hand signals, and not bark. Clipper had the inside of his left ear tattooed with his military serial number, 12X3, then was shipped to Vietnam to join the 44th Scout Dog Platoon near the Cambodian border.

When nineteen-year-old soldier John Burnam entered the dog kennel, he felt an immediate connection to the good-looking shepherd strutting about his run. Clipper's sharp eyes reflected intelligence, and his sleek black and brown coat shone as only a healthy dog's fur would. Burman requested to be paired with 12X3.

The soldier had already served as an infantryman and earned a Purple Heart. He had been wounded in action after jumping from a helicopter into a field of tall elephant grass and landing on a sharpened piece of bamboo called a *punji* stake that an enemy fighter had planted. Once his badly damaged knee healed, Burnam returned to Vietnam as a dog handler and joined the 44th Scout Dog Platoon.

He began training Clipper for real life combat missions. First, he taught the dog to alert him for trip wires. Enemy guerrillas would attach a trip wire to a hand grenade or bomb and conceal the device in the thick jungle vegetation. When a soldier unknowingly walked through the wire, it tripped the grenade or bomb, which exploded with deadly force.

To prepare for their first training session, Burnam strung a thin green wire between two rubber trees, about dog-nose high. He played with Clipper and cleaned the kennel run as usual, then put a work harness on the dog and headed to the area where he'd placed the trip wire. Clipper walked right through it.

The soldier snapped the leash back. "No, Clipper," he said sternly. "No." He bent down on one knee and tapped the wire on the dog's nose. He got eye-to-eye with the dog and asked what would happen if Clipper failed to alert him to the trip wire in a real-life situation. "BOOM!" he cried. "That's right. BOOM!"[1]

Clipper did not get the message right away. Dog and soldier repeated this exercise until both grew weary. Then, at the end of a long day of training, Clipper finally stopped at the wire and sat at attention. Relieved, Burnam hugged and praised the dog. In Vietnam scout dogs never received treats or toys out in the field. They worked for love and praise.

The next day Burnam planted many wires in lots of different locations, all the while observing Clipper's response and his body language for each alert. Watching Clipper gave Burnam a sense of the dog's thought patterns, movements, and reactions. At distances of thirty feet away, Clipper froze and refused to move forward, even when commanded. The dog gave different alerts for human and animal threats. He alerted from a greater distance while working in open fields, and shorter distances when in thick jungle vegetation.

Back at base camp, Burnam and Clipper practiced with all kinds of decoys and in all kinds of weather. When ordered to search, the dog moved to the full length of the six-foot leash, following his nose, forging a safe path. Burnam kept a keen eye on him, knowing that an alert lasted a few seconds or less before the dog moved on.

When Clipper sensed any decoy in the woods, his head and neck rose, his ears pointed sharply up, his mouth shut, and he froze momentarily. On strong alerts, the dog turned and looked to his handler. Burnam dropped to one knee, looked toward the direction of the alert, and silently hand-signaled the troops following behind of the danger ahead. They practiced until they responded to each other's cues, as flawless and in sync as professional dance partners. The dog responded to the motions of the soldier and the soldier followed the movements of the dog. Soon Clipper worked like radar on four paws.

Every morning Burnam opened Clipper's run. The dog always charged out, loped past his partner, and headed for his favorite tree. Burnam hooked Clipper's dog collar to a twenty-foot leash anchored to a tree, filled the dog's tin bucket with fresh water, and headed back to the kennels to clean Clipper's run.

One day, Burnam nailed a plaque to the tree and wrote CLIPPER in large block letters. In small print underneath the dog's name he wrote: "War is Good Business. Invest Your Dog."[2] It was Burnam's way of expressing his appreciation for the decision of Clipper's family to send their beloved pet to Vietnam.

Not every day was routine. Whenever Burnam appeared loaded up with over sixty pounds of supplies and ammunition for a combat mission, Clipper jumped around and barked excitedly. He knew from the soldier's gear that this day he would leave the base camp and work in the jungle. There were no front lines in Vietnam like there had been in World War II. Danger lurked everywhere outside of base camp, hiding in trees, in tall grasses, even under the ground. Once they went outside the safety of their camp, many lives depended on them.

On Clipper's first helicopter ride, flying 100 miles an hour above the jungle treetops, the dog stood forward on all fours with his nose outside the open door, taking in big gulps of air. His eyes squinted as his tongue flapped in the wind. Burnam held the leash in his hand with his arm extended to the limit. When Burnam's arm grew weary, he pulled Clipper back inside. Tired of having a sore arm afterward, he decided to teach his partner a lesson. Instead of letting the dog extend to the full length of the leash, he held on to a foot of slack. When Clipper stretched his leash to the limit, Burnam released the slack, causing the dog to

Clipper enjoyed taking in smells from the outdoors, but he learned to stay away from the open door of a moving helicopter.

fall forward frighteningly close to the open door. Clipper dropped to the ground and scooted back to Burnam as fast as he could. Lesson learned. After that the dog stayed close to his handler and away from open helicopter doors.

Green smoke billowed in the air, signaling it was safe to land the helicopter. As soon as they landed in enemy territory the troops headed for the cover of the trees. Landing on an open field and getting out of a chopper left the dog and the troops vulnerable to attack.

Their mission was to locate enemy base camps. The thickness of the tropical jungle required the dog team to closely follow a soldier with a machete. Rain poured down and mixed with the soldiers' sweat, while blood trickled from bug bites and thorny bushes. Insects chirped and birds tweeted as the machete sliced a path through the vegetation. Foot-long centipedes, fire ants, and blue and red lizards slinked underfoot. Leeches clung to the soldier's skin — but the troops had to keep moving, keep searching.

Burnam asked to take the point so that his dog could be more effective. Clipper led the way through the jungle, and soon gave a weak alert by flicking his ears and cocking his head. After another hundred yards, his ears shot straight up and he turned to Burnam. All the soldiers went down on one knee in response to the strong alert.

A few soldiers searched the area and discovered footprints. Clipper moved out and excitedly followed a scent trail that led to a deserted enemy base camp and a pile of hand grenades.

Burnam praised Clipper with a big hug and whispered, "Good dog, good dog." The soldiers destroyed the grenades and the commanding officer radioed the location of the camp so it would be demolished with air strikes.

On their return to K-9 camp, the soldiers walked in single file behind Clipper. Later, the lieutenant in charge thanked Burnam for a job well done and informed him that the dog team had earned a Bronze Star Medal for saving lives. (Though official military policy had ended the awarding of medals to dogs in 1944, individual units were allowed to continue the practice.)

"After you and your dog changed direction several times, my men got wise to what was going on, so they started searching for booby traps," the lieutenant said. In the end, the search had uncovered land mines, artillery shells, and trip wires.[3]

The lieutenant gave the dog a hug and put out his hand. "Shake," he said. Much to his handler's surprise, the dog placed his paw in the lieutenant's hand, and they shook.[4]

In between missions, Burnam groomed and played with his dog, and the two continued to practice. At the end of each day, he relaxed by playing cards and volleyball with the other dog handlers.

Burnam was soon promoted to sergeant. As the war raged on, he and Clipper continued to uncover booby traps, land mines, and even some enemy combatants. Unfortunately, the many miles of tracking through the jungle, carrying loads of survival supplies and ammunition, had taken a toll on Burnam's bum knee. As his limp grew more and more obvious, he was ordered to see an orthopedic surgeon at the medical facility in Cu Chi, a large base camp many miles away from the 44th Scout Dog Platoon. Burnam flew by helicopter to his doctor's appointment, missing the familiarity of holding Clipper by the end of his leash.

The doctor recommended that the soldier's leg be immobilized for a month — no running, no crawling, no jumping, and no marching. Burnam only had two months left on his tour of duty, so the doctor insisted he stay in Cu Chi to remain under medical observation until his tour was over.

Some combat soldiers would have welcomed this news, but to Burnam it proved devastating. He wouldn't be able to say goodbye to Clipper. His heart ached with thoughts of never seeing his buddy again. Staying in the hospital depressed him even more.

Burnam requested a helicopter ride to visit Clipper. His boss, a sergeant major, denied the request, ruling that his duty as a scout dog handler had ended.

Burnam couldn't accept the fact that he would return to the United States without ever seeing his partner again. The pain in his leg didn't compare to the unbearable pain in his heart. He thought that leaving a child behind couldn't feel any worse than abandoning Clipper.[5]

One day the sergeant major offered Burnam a deal. He needed an experienced combat sergeant to be the convoy master for a resupply mission. The convoy of tractors pulling empty trailers would have to travel back and forth on narrow winding jungle roads through miles of enemy territory. The sergeant major promised Burnam that if he accepted the mission — and survived — he could visit his old base camp to see Clipper.

Without hesitation, Burnam agreed to lead the convoy. From that moment on, he could think only of Clipper.

He envisioned playing with his dog, rolling around and wrestling with him. He remembered how Clipper sat down beside him and leaned all of his weight against the soldier's leg when he was tired.

The supply mission was a success and Burnam boarded the helicopter bound for Dau Tieng and the K-9 camp. As soon as he landed, he rushed to the kennels. Clipper was taking a nap under his tree. The soldier called to the dog. Clipper jumped up and raced over, tail wagging wildly, licking Burnam's face. In his excitement, Clipper piddled on the soldier's's leg and boots. Burnam didn't mind at all. Tears streamed down his face.

He unhooked Clipper and they went for a walk. The dog instinctively took his place by Burnam's left side and looked up, awaiting orders. After their walk they spent the rest of the day relaxing in the shade of the rubber trees.

Burnam had to return to Cu Chi the next morning. Before leaving, he cleaned Clipper's kennel, gave him a clean bucketful of water, and sat down under the tree with his partner. As he stroked the dog's head, he thought back to all of their missions. How many lives had this dog saved during their time together?

Burnam knew Clipper would make a wonderful pet, but orders were orders. He was going home, and Clipper still had a job to do.

The soldier stood and tore down the sign that read, "War is Good Business. Invest Your Dog," and angrily broke it into pieces. Clipper looked up and cocked his head. Burnam gave him one last hug and, with tears in his eyes, turned and walked away, leaving behind a part of himself.[6]

*John Burnam and Clipper patrolling the
Vietnam-Cambodia border in 1967.*

He never saw Clipper again. And Clipper never saw his family in California again.

The U.S. military had retrained and returned 6,000 Dogs for Defense to their owners following World War II, but it did an about-face in the Vietnam War. Military working dogs were deemed expendable and were ordered left behind. Officials cited several reasons — the cost involved, the possibility of disease transmission, the belief that the dogs were too vicious for civilization — but there was no evidence that any of these had been problems after World War II.

In the end, the military decided a dog was no different than a rifle — use it up, then dispose of it.

Clipper died in Vietnam. Of the approximately 5,000 dogs that served there, only 204 came home, including Nemo. The canine corps saved an estimated 10,000 lives during the war and about 232 dogs had made the ultimate sacrifice. Instead of being rewarded with happy retirements back home, many military dogs were either abandoned or euthanized in Vietnam. It remains the only U.S. war in which surviving military working dogs were left behind.[7]

"Clipper deserved to live the rest of his life in a peaceful environment away from that war," John Burnam would write in his memoir, *A Soldier's Best Friend*. "I wanted Clipper to be treated with the same dignity and respect I expected for myself. He had earned it. I knew as I sat under that tree with him leaning against my leg that I'd never see him again in this life. The tragedy of it all haunted me like a nightmare."[8]

CHAPTER NINE

ROBBY'S LAW

By the 1970s, terrorists had become skilled at planting small but deadly explosive devices in crowded cities, then sneaking off to detonate them. The U.S. military realized that homemade bombs could pose a threat to soldiers anywhere in the world and began training its canine corps to sniff for explosives.

For years the Lackland School had held campaigns urging the public to donate their dogs for defense, but by the 1990s very few dogs were being donated. And many of those were disqualified for medical or temperamental reasons. One year there were 802 new dogs at the beginning of training, but only 332 graduated. So Lackland decided to breed its own pups.[1]

In 1998 the Defense Department started the Military Working Dog Breeding Program at Lackland. Air Force Sgt. Thomas Edward Hawkinson, who was put in charge of the program, recommended the Belgian Malinois and German shepherd as the two best breeds for military working dogs. He had run tests that showed these breeds had amazing

Above: John Burnam with Clipper. After Burnam returned to the U.S., the military made the decision to leave Clipper and thousands of other military working dogs behind.

Below: Robby W005's gravestone. Robby and the World War II hero Chips are both interred at Hartsdale Pet Cemetery, Hartsdale, New York. The cemetery also has one of the earliest war dog memorials in the U.S., dedicated after World War I.

strength and endurance and excelled both at detecting materials and apprehending suspects. They could sniff out the bombs and track the terrorist who put them there.[2] The Labrador retriever also obtained high marks as a tracker dog. All of these breeds were known for making trustworthy and loyal partners — for no matter how talented the dog, it all came down to the friendship.

***

After the Vietnam War thousands of loyal, hard-working dogs like Clipper were left behind. His handler, John Burnam, is haunted by this decision to this day.

"Because our government had classified Clipper and all of the scout dogs as expendable equipment, I had to leave him behind," he wrote in his memoir. "I felt as if I were abandoning a brother.... How can my country burden me down with this life-long memory?"[3]

Then in 2000, the plight of a military working dog named Robby forced the government to right this wrong. Robby W005 was an eleven-year-old Belgian Malinois suffering from a chronic illness that had all but crippled him. He was in obvious pain. His handler wanted to adopt him, but the military rules didn't allow that.

Congressman Roscoe Bartlett read about Robby in a newspaper, and vowed to change the rules. He introduced a bill, known as "Robby's Law," that allowed retired military working dogs to be adopted by law enforcement agencies, their former handlers, or anyone else deemed capable of caring for them. Had Robby's Law existed during the Vietnam War, the government would have been required

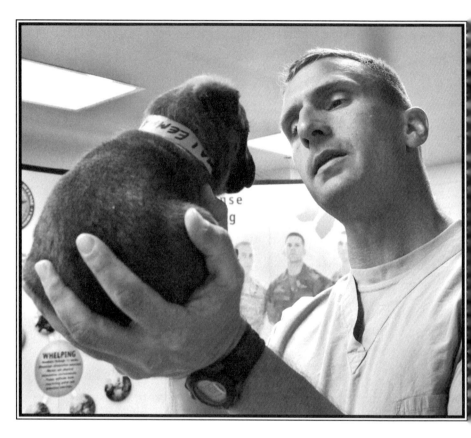

Army Sgt. 1st Class Russell Minta of the Military Working Dog Breeding Program on Lackland AFB, with a puppy. Lackland breeds only Belgian Malinois dogs.

to return any military working dogs that had been promised a home back in the United States.

The bill was rushed through both houses of Congress and passed without a single "no" vote. President Clinton signed it into law on January 24, 2000.[4]

With the enactment of Robby's Law, military working dogs are put up for adoption through a program at Lackland Air Force Base. Some of the dogs are older and have health issues like arthritis. Others suffer from post-traumatic stress disorder (PTSD), just as their human counterparts do. PTSD was not officially recognized in dogs until early 2011, after doctors began noting signs such as hyper-vigilance, greater "startle response," fleeing, and changes in the bond with the handler.

Despite these issues, people continue to line up to adopt these soldier dogs. "The list of applicants is eighteen months to two years long, because that many people want one of our dogs," said Colleen McGee from Lackland Air Force Base. "It's wonderful."[5]

CHAPTER TEN

REX

Detecting bombs had been a part of the military's dog training program for decades by the time of Operation Iraqi Freedom (2003-2011), but now it took on new importance. One of the biggest threats to the safety of American troops in Iraq was improvised explosive devices, or IEDs. Made at home with explosive ingredients and spare parts, they soon became the preferred weapon of guerrilla fighters, or insurgents, who wanted the U.S. military out of Iraq. When buried just below street level, an IED can destroy an armored vehicle and kill the soldiers inside. IEDs were responsible for two out of every three casualties (deaths and injuries) in Operation Iraqi Freedom.[1]

In Iraq, dog teams proved themselves so effective in their ability to locate fighters and ammunition that they became a prime target of enemy fire. Insurgents tried to stay a step ahead of the dog teams by finding different ingredients with which to make bombs. Another ploy to avoid detection was the use of herbs and other strong scents in bomb assemblies.

U.S. Marine Lance Cpl. Nick Lacarra and Coot, a Labrador retriever trained to detect improvised explosive devices (IEDs), on patrol in the Helmand province of Afghanistan in 2012.

Destined to become a war dog, Rex came to the United States as a puppy from one of Germany's top breeders. After living with a host family, the German shepherd arrived at Lackland Air Force Base on his first birthday. Early in his training Rex learned how to respond to silent hand signals for the basic commands: sit, stay, down, and heel. He practiced chasing and bringing down handlers who played the bad guys in bite-proof padded suits.

Rex followed his nose and located different components of explosives which were hidden around the dog school grounds. His reward for a job well done was always the same: a tennis ball or a Kong, a snowman-shaped dog chew made of hard rubber. To a high-energy dog, gnawing on one of these toys equaled pure bliss.

He passed military school with an impressive evaluation: *Rex is an independent dog who will search of his own accord if the handler allows it. He has excellent odor recognition and will track the odor until he pinpoints the source. He will respond regardless of the handler's position, and has had significant drop-leash and off-leash work.*[2]

Then he went to Camp Pendleton in California to await his handler, Corporal Mike Dowling, who was still training at Lackland.

Dowling's education began with his giving commands to an ammunition bucket filled with concrete. He spoke to the bucket using a high-pitched, energetic voice when he wanted to give praise. He used an authoritative voice when barking out commands, and he switched to a deep, menacing voice when wanting to establish himself as "pack leader." At first he felt foolish talking to a bucket, but after a while it almost seemed normal. Dowling and the other trainees practiced holding and handling a leash as if a military working dog stood on the other end of it.

Eventually he was paired with Argo, a Belgian Malinois who was also being trained. They practiced searching for explosive ingredients in mock airports, military barracks, vehicles, and buildings scattered about the grounds. Dowling adored Argo, who gave him his first taste of the bond between dog and handler.

After his training was complete, Dowling flew to Camp Pendleton to meet Rex. When he entered the kennel, he approached the shepherd, talking softly. Rex eyed the stranger warily. The dog's hair stood up on his back — a clear sign of aggression. Dowling continued to move toward Rex, showing no fear. He reached around the dog's neck to secure a leather collar that was attached to a leash.

When Dowling turned to reach for a choke collar, Rex lunged. He bared his teeth at the soldier, his jaws snapping. Dowling didn't waste a moment. He tackled the snarling canine and wrestled it to the ground. Then, putting his full weight on the dog to hold him down, Dowling wrapped the leash around Rex's jaw several times until it was shut tight.

Now came the moment of truth. Dowling put his head to the ground, next to Rex's face, and shouted in a commanding voice, "Out! Out! Out!"

When confronted with an aggressive dog, the handler is to do an "alpha roll" — show the animal who's boss and establish the human as the leader of the pack. The command "Out! Out! Out!" means only one thing to an

American military dog — *Stop what you're doing, right now*! If a handler does not establish his leadership immediately and firmly with an aggressive dog, the two will never work together.[3]

Here, however, handler and dog played their parts to perfection. Rex stopped growling and submitted to Dowling as the new alpha dog. From that point on, Rex would not only work for his pack leader, he would do anything to protect him.

From the beginning, Dowling vowed to be the best partner ever to Sergeant Rex. He fed the dog by hand and carefully groomed his thick German shepherd fur. "Regular grooming is part of the physical closeness you need to bond with your dog, where you and he become as one," Dowling wrote in his memoir, *Sergeant Rex*. "It's one of the most powerful signs of affection a handler can share with his dog."[4]

Some days Dowling ran Rex through the obstacle course to stay fit, ready to handle challenging circumstances. Rex spent other days sniffing for bomb materials hidden by Dowling. When Rex stiffened and raised his tail and head, it was a signal to Dowling that he was on the trail of something suspicious. Then his nose trailed along the ground, sucking in scents like a vacuum cleaner. When he found his treasure, the dog made one loud snort. Then he sat, statue-like, and stared.

Dowling knew the dog's detection stares. Rex's accuracy at finding explosives had been certified at more than 95 percent. This was huge, because there was one thing a soldier knew for sure — the real thing could kill you.[5]

Rex chases a "bad guy" in a bite-proof padded suit during a
training exercise.

A year and a half after their hard-and-fast introduction, Mike Dowling and Rex were one of the first war dog teams deployed to Iraq. They left Camp Pendleton on March 19, 2004, along with other battle-ready dog teams. Twelve dogs and twelve soldiers boarded the cargo plane to settle in for their twenty-six-hour flight. Dowling ordered Rex to "kennel up," then put his headphones on and sat in front of Rex's crate. He would keep an eye on his dog, and his dog could keep an eye on him.

The soldier tried not to focus on his fear of flying. He turned up the volume on his CD player, hoping the music would distract him. When that didn't work, he lay down close to the dog crate and drifted into a fitful slumber.

Along with the other dog teams, they were heading for an area of Iraq known as the "Triangle of Death" for all of the IEDs that had exploded there. The plane had a stopover in the United States before departing for Germany, then on to its final destination.

Eventually the C-17's cabin lights went out and dim red lights came on. This was a signal to the soldiers that they were now in Iraqi airspace — the war zone. The soldiers put on their bulletproof vests and secured vests on their dogs.

The huge plane zig-zagged its way across the sky to avoid ground fire, then took a nosedive out of the clouds before making a sharp landing at the Al-Asad air base in northern Iraq. Corporal Dowling's stomach spun and his throat tightened. He patted Rex, trying to calm his own nerves. Everyone disembarked into a hazy whiteness caused by the bright sun and got their first blast of extreme Middle East heat.

Their journey wasn't over. Dowling and Rex were assigned temporary quarters in a warehouse surrounded by a large fence while they awaited their marching orders. Dowling remembered that it felt like living on a chicken farm. He learned they had been assigned to Camp Mahmoudiyah, a dusty little Marine base near some of the worst IED activity in Iraq.

They sat in the back of military trucks, riding through the endless desert sand. The Iraqi sun beat down on them. Sweat beaded on Dowling's face. Rex stood panting in the open air. Dust billowed from the dirt roads, filling the soldiers' noses with a mixture of desert sand and dirt.

As Dowling approached the gate of Mahmoudiyah, fear consumed him, making it difficult to breathe. As if sensing his handler's distress, Rex looked up and gave him a confident look. The dog seemed to be telling him: *If you're here, that's good enough for me.*[6]

That reassured Dowling, but the uneasy feeling returned once they got inside the base. No one, it seemed, was expecting a dog to show up. Canine corps had not been used by Americans in combat since the Vietnam War. Some of the Marines that Dowling met told him they had no idea dogs were being used to sniff out bombs.

The commanding officer showed Dowling where Rex was to sleep — in separate quarters from his handler. Dowling explained that he was never apart from his partner, and if they were to be an effective team, it needed to stay that way. The commanding officer was surprised but granted permission for Dowling to find new sleeping quarters.[7]

He located a small concrete hut beneath the watchtower with no windows, no electricity, and no air conditioning. It was next to a garbage dumpster and a noisy generator. Dowling called it "the bunker." There was a single tree beside the building. The tree would provide shade for Rex and a place to relieve himself. This was home.

One morning, Dowling stepped out of the bunker to find General James Mattis, the overall commander of the U.S. Marine Corps, standing outside. Startled, Dowling turned to Rex and ordered: "Heel! Sit! Stay!"

The general flashed a huge grin.

"Well, if it isn't a dog team!" he told Dowling. "You're the first Marine Corps canine team I've seen in Iraq." The three-star general bent down to pet Rex, but Dowling thrust out his hand.

"Sir," he said, "with all due respect, he's a working dog, and I don't want to risk an accidental bite."

The general laughed and backed off.

"You know, no device on earth can measure up to a dog's nose when he's looking for explosives," said the commander. "You guys stay safe out there."[7]

***

Inside the bunker, Rex and Dowling waited for an assignment. And waited. Dowling groomed and played with his partner. They did bomb-detection drills to keep Rex's sniffer well-tuned. Day after day, however, they were assigned gate duty, and day after day reports filtered in of soldiers and Humvees from the base being blown up by IEDs.

Dowling's frustration boiled over. He asked permission to speak to the first sergeants in charge. He brought Rex along to plead his case. He discovered that the sergeants had no idea there was a dog team on base. Living in the bunker, away from the main barracks, Dowling and Rex had been invisible.

The sergeants were thrilled to learn about this four-footed IED detector at their disposal. Dog and handler were ordered to start their work that evening, clearing roads for a convoy of Humvees.

The Second Battalion of the Second Marines had been relying on metal detectors to locate IEDs. But those machines couldn't tell between a metal that was inert and one that could explode. Rex could tell the difference. He and Dowling spent the next few months clearing the area of countless IEDs, making the Triangle of Death safe for travel again.

One day they were en route to Fallujah, a hotbed of insurgent activity, when their convoy of trucks and Humvees came under attack. As machine-gun fire hammered away, Dowling and Rex scrambled out of their vehicle and headed for a protective berm alongside the road. The soldier ordered the dog to lie down flat — and then he lay on top of Rex, protecting the dog with his body. Rex took it all very calmly. His cool demeanor helped Corporal Dowling relax as the firefight raged around them.

On another assignment, they were ordered to join the Second Battalion on a farm outside of Fallujah that was suspected of being an insurgent hideout. American F-15 jets thundered overhead to provide cover for the dog team as they inspected the zone. This would be a long day; Rex's nose would be working overtime.

Dowling did what he often did at the start of a grueling assignment: he took hold of his dad's rosary beads and pushed a small carved stone bear deep into his pocket, the one his mom had offered for safety and protection. Then he flashed the red Kong in his pocket. He knew Rex would do anything for a chance to play with his rubber chew toy.

Despite the distraction of jet engines, Rex hit paydirt early and often. He signaled his first hit inside one of the buildings. Dowling summoned other Marines to the spot where his dog waited silently, and soon they had uncovered a large stash of machine guns.

Out in the fields, Rex suddenly stopped sniffing and parked himself on the ground. Marines came to the spot and started digging. Deep in the dirt, insurgents had buried several four-foot-long rocket propelled grenades, or RPGs.

Another field yielded more RPGs along with bomb-making materials. By the end of the day the dog team had cleared the area of hundreds of weapons and explosives.

The base's second-in-command called Rex a "superstar."[9] But there would be no superstar treatment for this soldier dog — just more chances to play with the Kong.

Another team joined Dowling and Rex to help clear several miles of a road to Fallujah that had been rocked by IED explosions. Then the teams searched buildings and vehicles in Fallujah. There are no public records on how many lives were saved during Operation Iraqi Freedom, but one source estimated that each dog saved from 150 to 1,800 lives during its service.[10]

After seven months of nonstop duty, Dowling got the call he had been dreading. His father was losing his battle with cancer. The corporal requested leave to go home and be with his family to spend one last Christmas with his dad. By this time, however, Rex E168 was too valuable to the Marines to wait in a kennel for Dowling's return. So he was assigned to a new handler, Cpl. Megan Leavey. The two worked more than 100 missions together.

By 2006 dog teams had become so successful at eliminating the IED threat that enemy fighters began targeting the dogs. In September of that year, Leavey and Rex were on a patrol in Ramadi when a blast erupted beneath their feet. It's believed the device was triggered by an Iraqi insurgent who was watching the dog team from a nearby rooftop. Leavey suffered a traumatic brain injury and was eventually discharged from the Marines, but Rex recovered and was assigned to a new handler and went back to sniffing for bombs.

In 2012 Cpl. Leavey learned that Rex had contracted a disease that had robbed him of much of his olfactory powers. He was back in Camp Pendleton, sitting in a kennel. Leavey petitioned the Marine Corps to adopt her old partner and give him a pleasant retirement at her home in New York. The Marines said no. Under Robby's Law, the military had the right to refuse an adoption request. Leavey went to the news media.

"Rex is my partner. I love him," she told MSNBC. "He is ready to be retired."[11]

Veterans' groups and New York senator Charles E. Schumer joined the campaign to let Leavey adopt Rex.

More than 21,000 dog lovers signed an online petition. Finally the Marines relented, and this distinguished veteran of Operation Iraqi Freedom was let out of his kennel. Sergeant Rex lived out his final months in the care of his handler.

Rex, a chew toy, and his handler Megan Leavey at Rex's retirement and open adoption ceremony at Camp Pendleton, Calif., April 6, 2012. In addition to detecting IEDs, Rex took part in more than 6,000 vehicle inspections in Iraq.

CHAPTER ELEVEN

GABE

If Sergeant Rex was the upper-crust officer with the best breeding, upbringing, and education, then Gabe was the street-smart grunt from the school of hard knocks. The first three years of this yellow Labrador retriever's life were spent roaming the alleys of Houston, Texas, scrounging for food and fighting for respect.

Every evening he found a safe place to rest until one night his luck ran out. The dog was captured and carried off to the city's "kill shelter," so called because animals not adopted within thirty days were euthanized there.

Fortunately, the Southeast Texas Labrador Retriever Rescue Organization soon learned about the newest inmate at the dog pound. The group passed the word on to Lackland Air Force Base, where the Specialized Search Dog Program was looking for recruits.

Labrador retrievers had excelled in search-and-rescue division in the Vietnam War, which meant this dog, given the name of Gabe, had the potential to make a great soldier for the war in Iraq.

Unfortunately, that potential was not on display during Gabe's first weeks of search-dog school. He moped about the kennel, uninterested in pleasing anyone. When commanded to sit, he stood. When told to "come," he sat. "He was being a dog," said his handler, Sergeant First Class Charles Shuck. "He just didn't want to search, didn't want to find stuff."[1]

Still, Sgt. Shuck couldn't resist the sweet dog whose survival story had been passed along by the dog catcher. "I fell in love with Gabe from the start," he said. So he tried to work with Gabe's unusual personality. "He's never been a very hyper dog," said Shuck. "He's very personable."[2]

After five months of training Gabe had made progress, but another dog at the school, named Doki, seemed to perform better in the simulated search-and-rescue drills.

The time came for the final trial to be held in real-world conditions at a training ground in Arizona. Only the highest-performing dogs at the trials would be selected for overseas deployment. Shuck braced himself for disappointment.

"I didn't think Gabe was going to be my dog," he recalled. "I liked him more than the other dog personally, but I had to take the dog that would save my life downrange."

It was like Gabe had read his mind. The mellow retriever suddenly kicked it up several notches and went on to dominate the trials. Shuck was amazed. "You'd think he knew that if he didn't perform, he wasn't going with me," he said. "Gabe actually performed like a rock star and Doki was scared of the dark."[3]

Now an official military working dog, Gabe had the serial number K153 tattooed in his left ear. In August 2006, he and Sgt. Shuck boarded a plane with other soldiers of the 178th Military Police Detachment, headed for Mosul, Iraq. There they spent nearly every day searching roadsides and riverbanks for hidden bombs and ammunition.

Shuck would let Gabe off his leash and the dog would "walk point" about 100 yards ahead of his handler and the rest of the soldiers. Whenever he came upon a suspicious scent he would sit down, alerting the troops behind him to the dangers ahead.

"It's Gabe's job to find the bad stuff before the bad stuff finds the soldiers," said Shuck.[4]

The dog never did get used to the sound of gunfire — even from one hundred yards away, his handler could see Gabe's body shaking when there was shooting nearby — but he stayed on task. A search dog needs only fifteen minutes to clear an area that takes a foot soldier more than an hour to clear. They combed through scorching hot desert, farmland, and rock-strewn hills. They rummaged through villages, homes, cars, and security checkpoints.

While walking point along the steep banks of the Tigris River, Gabe gave the danger signal and soldiers unearthed one of their biggest hauls yet, enough explosives to create dozens of IEDs. Every night the reward for saving lives was the same — a chance to chew on a tennis ball and a Kong.

The soldiers on base enjoyed wrestling and playing with the retriever. "Gabe was a piece of home to them," Shuck said. "They'd left their families behind. They'd left their dogs behind. For them to just put their face in Gabe's fur for a few seconds would take them back home — and get them

Gabe and Sgt. Shuck on patrol. In Iraq, they uncovered more explosives and weapons in one year than any other dog team.

back where they needed to be." On their days off, Shuck and Gabe would visit the hospitals to cheer up wounded troops. Just as Smoky had lifted the spirits of the sick and wounded in World War II, Gabe was therapy to everyone from the nursing staff to the terminally ill.[5]

"If we were able to go over to the unit and let them cry on Gabe's fur and just go be the dog in that unit, we did that," said Shuck.[6]

Thirteen months after arriving in Mosul, the dog team finished their term of deployment. Gabe had gone on more than 200 combat missions and made 26 discoveries of explosives and weapons, more "finds" than any other search dog in Iraq that year.

The following year, back at Fort Hood in Texas, Shuck received orders to surrender Gabe to a new handler.

"It was horrifying," Shuck recalled. "I had to put him in the truck and shut the door and watch him get driven away to Lackland."

A few weeks later, however, Shuck took a call from an officer at Lackland. It seemed that Gabe had also found separation from his handler intolerable, and refused to work with anyone else. The officer asked if he would like to adopt Gabe.

"I'm not going to lie, I was very happy," said Shuck. "I wanted him to be at home with me, because that's where I knew he belonged. When he left, it was like a piece of my heart was taken out. I almost died."[7]

After Shuck adopted Gabe, the pair traveled around the country and the soldier spread the word about shelter dogs and war dogs. He encouraged people to adopt animals in shelters and to send much needed supplies to the soldier dogs and their handlers. Gabe's popular Facebook page helped place shelter animals in their forever homes.

In 2008, the American Kennel Club awarded Gabe the Heroic Military Working Dog Medal, an award that included animals from all of the armed forces. Gabe also earned three Army Commendation Medals, an Army Achievement Medal, and 40 coins of excellence.

For his service, the American Humane Association crowned Gabe with the 2012 Hero Dog Award. "It is vital that we honor and protect all our military heroes — at both ends of the leash," said Dr. Robin Ganzert, president and CEO of the American Humane Association. "Military working dogs have been a vital life-saving part of our armed services and they deserve our support when they can no longer work."[8]

Shuck donated the $15,000 prize money to the U.S. War Dog Association, which provides care packages with everything from rope chews to nail clippers to beef jerky for these four-footed soldiers and their handlers.

Gabe connected with the students at his numerous school visits. "When we were in Iraq, we wrote to a lot of kids ... about respect and all that stuff, staying in school, respecting each other, respecting their teachers," Shuck said. "If there's twenty kids in the room and if we (keep) one of these kids from doing the wrong thing, then we've done our job that day."[9]

When ten-year-old Gabe refused to eat for the first time in his life, a veterinarian discovered incurable cancer in the dog's spleen and liver. Surrounded by his favorite toys and all of his medals, he was put to sleep on February 13, 2013. "Gabe took his last breath at 12:44 p.m. while I held him in my arms," Shuck wrote on his Facebook page.[10]

Thousands of sympathy messages poured in from around the world for Gabe, the pound puppy turned military working dog.

Chuck Shuck and Gabe, sporting their medals.

EPILOGUE

Pfc. Rez P. Hester of the Marine Corps Seventh War Dog Platoon on Iwo Jima takes a nap while Butch stands guard in February 1945.

So much has changed since the first mascot dogs wandered onto the battlefield and into the hearts of American soldiers. Over the years these canine companions have put their superhuman powers to work on behalf of their handlers — sounding the alarm, detecting poison gas, finding bomb ingredients, and tracking down ever-more-elusive enemies. In turn, the military has learned to produce a more highly-skilled working dog than ever. From humble beginnings in 1958, the military working dog school at Lackland Air Force Base in Texas has developed specialized training for the different branches of the military, an active breeding program, even a new $15 million, state-of-the-art dog hospital on base.

In 2010 the director of the Pentagon's effort to counter the threat of IEDs made a startling admission. Lt. Gen. Michael Oates said that the Defense Department had spent $19 billion on high-tech innovations to identify roadside bombs. After all that, he said, the Pentagon had concluded that the best weapon against IEDs was still a military working dog and its handler.[1]

There may be no better example of today's canine corps than Cairo, a Belgian Malinois assigned to the top-secret Navy SEAL division. Navy SEALs have their own military schools for dogs. Along with their handlers, these elite canines are special ops experts, trained to perform on sea, air, and land, from scorching hot deserts to the Arctic. Taking photos of these dogs or their handlers is prohibited, and the skills they learn at Lackland are classified secrets.

Early in the morning of May 2, 2011, Cairo and his handler dropped out of a helicopter, along with 78 other commandos belonging to SEAL Team Six, on a bold raid that would make headlines around the globe. U.S. intelligence had determined that the person living inside a heavily fortified compound in Abbottabad, Pakistan, was most likely Osama bin Laden, mastermind of the 9/11 attacks that had killed nearly 3,000 Americans. The SEALs were going in to take bin Laden out, dead or alive. Cairo's job was to alert his handler if anyone entered the compound. The raid ended with bin Laden's death but no U.S. casualties.[2]

Many of the details of Operation Neptune Spear, as the bin Laden raid was called, have been kept secret. It's likely, though, that Cairo was wearing a bulletproof vest, "doggles" (protective goggles specially made for canine heads), and earbuds so that his handler could give commands into a microphone mounted on the soldier's vest. Cairo may also have been carrying a night vision camera on his back, adding an extra set of eyes and ears to the humans monitoring the raid.

It's easy to forget, though, that underneath all that specialized military gear is something that hasn't changed in thousands of years — the beating heart of a dog, one that is utterly devoted to its handler.

Some have not forgotten. For years, animal advocates and veterans continued to fight for the rights of military war dogs and worked to make improvements to Robby's Law. On January 2, 2013, President Obama put his signature on the Canine Members of the Armed Forces Act to reclassify the dogs from equipment to service members and to give them passage back home.[3]

Robby's Law had been passed without any funding, so families wanting to adopt the dogs had to foot the bill themselves. Congress corrected this as well, and in 2016 President Obama signed into law a bill that assigned money for transporting retired dogs back to the United States and providing for their veterinary care. Military working dogs who return from service in the future will also receive the same medical attention and care as their soldiers.[4]

After the dogs retire from active duty, groups like the U.S. War Dog Association, Warrior Dog Foundation,

Military Working Dog Foundation, and Mission K9 Rescue transition the dogs from the war zone into loving adoptive homes. Others begin new careers in law enforcement as bomb-sniffing, drug-detecting, or sentry dogs. And still others become therapy and service dogs, giving support and comfort to those who need it most. It's an increasingly important job at a time when post-traumatic stress is being recognized as perhaps the most serious of all war wounds.

***

Ron Aiello still thinks of his partner Stormy every day. Aiello, a Vietnam veteran who serves as president of the U.S. War Dog Association, credits Stormy with saving his life on numerous occasions by alerting him to snipers and booby traps.

Aiello has been on a mission to restore military honors for acts of canine valor. Individual units have awarded Purple Hearts to dogs wounded in combat, but no medals for dogs have been officially sanctioned since the Chips controversy in World War II brought an end to the practice.[5]

"To this day Cairo, Stubby, and all of the military working dogs have yet to be formally recognized by the United States military, despite having served multiple tours or being injured or killed in action," said Sen. Robert Menendez of New Jersey, who introduced a bill to create a Guardians of America's Freedom Medal for military working dogs and their handlers.[6]

From Guam to California to New York, memorials and monuments to these noble warriors have been built by their grateful soldiers. The first official state memorial to honor military dogs and their handlers was dedicated June 10, 2006, in Holmdel, New Jersey. More recently, also in New Jersey, the veterans of Mount Olive built a memorial to five of the military working dogs featured in this book: Stubby, Smoky, Nemo, Gabe, and one of the life-saving Dobermans from World War II.

A campaign led by John Burnam persuaded the U.S. military to give its canine corps their own officially sanctioned national memorial. The Military Working Dog Teams National Monument was dedicated on October 28, 2013, at Lackland Air Force Base. The nine-foot bronze and granite monument displays a handler surrounded by dogs from the most prominent working breeds — Doberman

The Military Working Dog Teams National Monument at Lackland AFB.

pinscher, German shepherd, Labrador retriever, and Belgian Malinois. An inscription reads, "Dedicated to all U.S. Military Working Dog Handlers and their beloved dogs who defend America from harm, defeat the enemy, and save lives."

Before gunpowder and mechanization, dogs charged into battles as the first line of defense. Over time, as weaponry developed, the dogs carried goods, delivered messages, pulled sleds, and served sentry duty. As the wars became more sophisticated, the dogs became more specialized.

With hidden bombs the number one threat in today's conflicts, the demand for paws-on-the-ground continues to soar. Since 2001, the Pentagon has doubled the number of military working dogs trained each year. Currently an estimated 1,700 dogs from Lackland AFB are deployed around the world in both war and peace zones.[7]

By their side are 1,700 devoted handlers, all of whom feel incredibly lucky to have met their extraordinary best friend. Through the years, these handlers have learned to trust their partners' instincts with their very lives.

Military dogs not only save lives, they have saved the sanity of many a soldier. Dogs bring a bit of humanity in even the worst of times. The compassion, loyalty, emotional, and physical support given by dogs are the same qualities found in a best friend.

Without saying a word, dogs set an example for us to follow — greet the ones we love with enthusiasm, love unconditionally, be reliable, serve others, act unselfishly, and protect the ones we love.

Whether walking point, or beside us, in the battlefield of war or in the battlefield of life, there is nothing like a best friend, and there is nothing like a good dog.

Petty Officer 2nd Class Blake Soller and Rico, his military working dog, at the National War Dog Cemetery on Naval Base Guam. The memorial is to 25 war dogs, mostly Doberman pinschers, killed in the line of duty on Guam during World War II.

AUTHOR'S NOTE

I did not write this book alone. Two faithful companions lay by my side: Tessie, my Australian blue heeler, and Toby, my German shorthair pointer. Some days they snored loudly, but like good dogs, they were always there. As long as I can remember, I've had a dog in my life, always at least one but never more than three. For me, it is a soul connection. Dogs are family and best friend wrapped up in one furry bundle. I know firsthand the fierce love humans can feel for their canine companions, and I appreciate the powerful bond the soldiers described when they spoke of their military working dogs.

In 2007, a morning news show about Fluffy, an Iraqi street dog adopted by an American soldier, caught my attention. It was the first time I ever thought about a dog in the war zone, so I did some digging on the topic. I uncovered stories of mascot war dogs that helped the cause, but I also learned of the military working dogs that were specifically trained for combat.

Some people argue that dogs shouldn't be trained for warfare, but we sent our men and women into battle. In times of war, we suffer human and canine causalities, but that dog in the grave may have saved a soldier's life, or maybe even hundreds of lives. The heartwarming stories of these hard-working dogs and soldiers swayed me to believe that the dogs preferred to be at the side of their partners more than anyplace else in the world.

This nine-year journey from idea to published book started with a road trip to Vohne Liche Kennels in Indiana. Upon arrival, my dear friend Carol Neale and I hopped into a van with Ken Licklider and a few soldiers with military working dogs and we all headed for the training grounds. That morning we watched a group of dog teams running bomb detection drills. In the afternoon were obstacle drills. The day ended with a demonstration of a soldier in a bite suit being ferociously attacked by a dog. The dog not only attacked with impressive force, he also quickly stopped his aggression when ordered.

Although I took photos throughout the day, the commanding officer instructed me to delete them all since the teams we had observed were top secret weapons of our government and absolutely no photos were permitted. I respectfully complied.

Over the years, the humble, brave veterans I spoke with, or had the honor of meeting, were some of the most gracious, generous people I have ever known. One such veteran, Bill Wynne, met me at McDonald's with an 8-by-10 photo of his deceased wife, Margie. Right then and there I knew he was a gem of a man. He fought in World War II with Smoky, a Yorkshire terrier, by his side. His wife Margie would jokingly say of Bill's Yorkie, "The other woman was a real dog."

John Burnam's story came to life on a video called *War Dogs*. The heart-wrenching tale literally left me bawling. When I interviewed Bob Throneburg, his voice brimmed with pride when he spoke of Nemo, who saved his life and later starred in a recruitment effort for military war dogs.

Chuck Shuck shared some priceless memories of the friendship he shared with his golden retriever, Gabe. I marveled at the love and devotion these tough soldiers had for their dogs. Ron Aiello of the U.S. War Dog Association continues to fight for the rights of the military dogs to be officially honored with medals or awards for their bravery and service to our country.

My uncle, Donald Roe, remembers when he was just a young boy and his older brother Eddie, my dad, was overseas fighting in World War II. Uncle Don read an article in a Brooklyn newspaper about a military war dog that had saved the life of a soldier. The story moved him to tears. He clipped the article from the paper, shoved it deep into his pocket, and carried it around for years. Dogs have a way of pulling on our heart strings. Researching and writing this book confirms my belief that whether on the battlefront or the home front, a dog truly is man's best friend.

If you would like to supply much needed items for our military war dogs, visit the website of K-9 War Dog Advocates. There you can donate a variety of items from rope chews and dog bowls to doggles and booties.

***

Thank you, Tanya Anderson, for believing in me, for believing in this book, and for giving it an awesome title. I'd also like to thank my wonderful critique group in Columbus, Ohio — Margaret Peterson Haddix, Jenny Patton, Linda Gerber, Linda Stanek, Amjed Qamar, and Erin MacLellan — for reviewing many revisions. Thanks to my friend Karen Thorley for introducing me to Lt. Leslie

Reichardt and his family. Darrell Trent added many great details of the dogs and soldiers fighting in the Vietnam War. The staff of the Dublin branch of the Columbus Metropolitan Library steered me to lots of materials and offered many encouraging words.

Carol Neale, Donna Drake, Lindsay Pimm, and my sister Loraine Roe were my invaluable early readers. Special thanks to all of the veterans who shared their stories and information, including Chief Tim Murphy, Dave Brennan, Major Douglas Miller, and Major Kathy Jordan of Lackland AFB. Thank you to the amazing sculptor Susan Bahary for sharing the story of Captain William Putney. And my love and gratitude go out to my husband Ed Pimm for always being there for me. Last but not least, thanks to Quindaro Press for bringing history to life for the youth of today.

NOTES

INTRODUCTION: IT TAKES TWO

1   "Prussian and Powerful: What Made Frederick Great," *The Economist*, September 12, 2015.

2   Lemish, Michael, *War Dogs: A History of Loyalty and Heroism* (Washington: Brassey, 1996), 4.

3   Goodavage, Maria, *Soldier Dogs: The Untold Story of America's Canine Heroes* (New York: New American Library, 2013), 10.

4   "A Bin Laden Hunter on Four Legs," *New York Times*, May 4, 2011.

5   Bradshaw, John, *Dog Sense: How the New Science of Dog Behavior Can Make You a Better Friend* (New York: Basic, 2011), 233.

6   Tyson, Peter, "Dogs' Dazzling Sense of Smell," accessed at pbs.org/wgbh/nova/nature/dogs-sense-of-smell.html (November 16, 2016).

7   Mike Ritland, quoted in *60 Minutes,* Season 45 Episode 27, video posted April 21, 2013 to youtube.com/watch?v=FsnPAQ137fY (accessed November 16, 2016).

8   Goodavage, *Soldier Dogs*, 2.

9   Alaimo, Carol Ann, "Dogs of war are the most peaceable pooches," *Arizona Daily Star*, January 12, 2004, posted to freerepublic.com/focus/f-news/1319549/posts, accessed November 16, 2016.

10   Martin Sheen, narrator, *War Dogs: America's Forgotten Heroes* (Los Angeles: GRB Entertainment Video, 1999).

DOG JACK

1   Niebaum, John H., *History of the Pittsburgh Washington Infantry, 102nd* (Pittsburgh: Burgum Printing Co., 1931), 116-117.

2   Stewart, Alexander M., *Camp, March and Battle-field, or, Three years and a half with the Army of the Potomac* (Philadelphia: James B. Rodgers, 1865), 270-271.

3   Zucchero, Michael, *Loyal Hearts: Histories of American Civil War Canines* (Lynchburg, Va.: Schroeder Publications, 2011), 85.

4   Robertson, James, *The Untold Civil War: Exploring the Human Side of War* (Washington: National Geographic, 2011), 34.

5   "Old Abe, the War Eagle," Wisconsin Historical Society, accessed at wisconsinhistory.org.

6   Robertson, *Untold Civil War*, 124.

RINTY

1 "Cher Ami — World War I Carrier Pigeon," *Encyclopedia Smithsonian,* si.edu, accessed February 20, 2017.
2 Orlean, Susan, *Rin Tin Tin: The Life And the Legend* (New York: Simon & Schuster, 2011), 33ff.

STUBBY

1 Bausum, Ann, *Stubby the War Dog* (Washington: National Geographic, 2014), 17.
2 Bausum, Ann. *Sergeant Stubby: How a Stray Dog and His Best Friend Helped Win World War I and Stole the Heart of a Nation*, 48.
3 Bausum, *Stubby the War Dog*, 21.
4 Bausum, *Stubby the War Dog*, 21.
5 Brittain, Vera, *Testament of Youth: An Autobiographical Study Of The Years 1900-1925* (New York: Macmillan, 1933), 395.
6 Mott, Maryanne, "Dogs of War: Inside the U.S. Military's Canine Corps," *National Geographic News*, April 9, 2013, news.nationalgeographic.com.
7 Bausum, *Stubby the War Dog*, 22-29.
8 Kane, Gillian, "Sergeant Stubby," *Slate*, slate.com, accessed November 16, 2016.
9 "Georgetown Traditions: Jack The Bulldog," hoyasaxa.com/sports/bulldog.htm, accessed November 16, 2016.
10 Newton, Tom, "Sergeant Stubby, Over There!", k9history.com/WWI-sergeant-stubby.htm, accessed November 16, 2016.

SMOKY

1 Lemish, Michael, *War Dogs* (Washington, D.C.: Brassey, 1996), 30.
2 Wynne, William A., *Yorkie Doodle Dandy: A Memoir* (Denver: Top Dog, 1996), 1-2.
3 Author interview with William A. Wynne, April 1, 2016.
4 Author interview with William A. Wynne, May 25, 2011.
5 Author interview with William A. Wynne, February 17, 2016.
6 Information from Therapy Dogs International (tdi-dog.org, accessed November 16, 2016).
7 Wynne, *Yorkie Doodle Dandy*, 51.

SHOULD A DOG GET A SILVER STAR?

1 Interview with Susan Bahary, November 11, 2016.
2 Kelly, Kate, "Chips, First Dog Sent Overseas in World War II," *America Comes Alive*, americacomesalive.com, accessed November 16, 2016.

3   "Army Dog Is First To Win DSC Award," *New York Times*, January 14, 1944, 4.
4   "Medals for Everybody," *Time*, Feb. 28, 1944, time.com, accessed November 16, 2016.
5   "PDSA Dickin Medal for Lucca," pdsa.org.uk, accessed November 16, 2016.

ROGER WILCO

1   Reichardt, Leslie, "WWII Travels of Roger Wilco" (unpublished memoir), 1-4.
2   Unpublished letter by Leslie Reichardt shared with the author.

NEMO

1   General Orders 114, Headquarters, Eighth United States Army, Korea, 18 January 1953, uswardogs.org/war-dog-history/korean/, accessed November 16, 2016.
2   Lemish, *War Dogs*, 160.
3   "War Dogs of Vietnam," attributed to staff of Hahn AFB, Germany, b-29s-over-korea.com, accessed November 16, 2016.
4   Lemish, *Forever Forward*, 135.
5   Author interview with Robert Throneburg, May 24, 2016.
6   "AF Sentry Dog To Become Symbol Of Professionalism," Seventh Air Force News, August 9, 1967, tsna.org/7thafnews/aug091967. html, accessed December 17, 2016.
7   Lemish, *Forever Forward*, 135.
8   Author interview with Robert Throneburg, May 24, 2016.
9   Hahn AFB, "War Dogs of Vietnam."
10 Lemish, *Forever Forward*, 135.
11 Author interview with Robert Throneburg, May 24, 2016.

CLIPPER

1   Burnam, John C., *A Soldier's Best Friend: Scout Dogs and Their Handlers in the Vietnam War* (New York: Carroll & Graf, 2000), 230.
2   Burnam, John C., *Dog Tags of Courage: Combat Infantrymen And War Dog Heroes in Vietnam* (Fort Bragg: Lost Coast, 2000), 156.
3   Burnam, *A Soldier's Best Friend*, 254.
4   Burnam, *Dog Tags of Courage*, 203.
5   Burnam, *A Soldier's Best Friend*, 317.
6   Sheen, *War Dogs*.
7   McFarland, "Trustworthy Partners."
8   Burnam, *A Soldier's Best Friend*, 317.

ROBBY'S LAW

1   English, Tracy L., *The Quiet Americans: A History of Military Working Dogs* (San Antonio: Lackland AFB, 2000), 17.
2   English, *The Quiet Americans,* 23.
3   Burnam, *A Soldier's Best Friend*, 244.
4   Goodavage, *Soldier Dogs,* 247.
5   Epatko, Larisa, "Military Working Dogs: What Happens After They Serve?" *PBS NewsHour Online*, May 28, 2012, pbs.org/newshour.

REX

1   Zoroya, Gregg, "How the IED changed the U.S. military," *USA Today,* Dec. 18, 2013.
2   Dowling, Mike, *Sergeant Rex: The Unbreakable Bond Between a Marine and His Military Working Dog* (New York: Simon & Schuster, 2011), 74.
3   Dowling, *Sergeant Rex*, 78.
4   Dowling, *Sergeant Rex*, 30.
5   Dowling, *Sergeant Rex*, 23.
6   Dowling, *Sergeant Rex*, 117.
7   Dowling, *Sergeant Rex*, 13.
8   Dowling, *Sergeant Rex*, 19.
9   Dowling, *Sergeant Rex*, 166-177.
10 Goodavage, *Soldier Dogs,* 12.
11 Kari Huus, "Marine and dog bonded by war, divided by red tape," MSNBC.com, March 9, 2012, accessed November 16, 2016.

GABE

1   Collins, Elizabeth M., "Dog, Veteran, Hero," *Soldiers: The Official U.S. Army Magazine*, soldiers.dodlive.mil, accessed November 16, 2016.
2   Sturrock, Staci. "A hero on four legs: Gabe the military dog," *Palm Beach Post*, January 18, 2013, findagrave.com (grave ID 105204372), accessed November 16, 2016.
3   Collins, "Dog, Veteran, Hero."
4   Sturrock, "A hero on four legs."
5   Sturrock, "A hero on four legs."
6   Collins, "Dog, Veteran, Hero."
7   Collins, "Dog, Veteran, Hero."
8   Sturrock, "A hero on four legs."

9   Collins, "Dog, Veteran, Hero."

10 McBride, Wallace, "Iraq veteran, celebrated working dog Gabe passes away in his owner's arms," *Fort Jackson Leader*, February 21, 2013, army.mil, accessed November 16, 2016.

EPILOGUE

1   Frankel, Rebecca, "Military Dogs Sniff Out IEDs, Save Lives," *Wall Street Journal*, Oct 31, 2014.

2   Ritland, Mike, *Navy SEAL Dogs: My Tale of Training Canines for Combat* (New York: St. Martin's Griffin, 2013), 121.

3   The Canine Members of the Armed Forces Act was part of the National Defense Authorization Act (112th Congress, H.R. 4310).

4   Scarborough, Rowan, "New law facilitates military dogs return to U.S. adoption by battlefield handlers," *Washington Times*, November 30, 2015.

5   McFarland, Cynthia, "Trustworthy Partners," October 28, 2011, ocalastyle.com, accessed November 16, 2016.

6   Hopkins, Kathleen, "Menendez wants to honor 4-legged patriots," *Asbury Park Press*, June 11, 2016, app.com/story/news/2016/06/11/menendez-wants-honor-4-legged-patriots/85701254/ (November 16, 2016).

7   Information supplied by Operations Staff, Lackland AFB, email dated November 20, 2016.

PHOTO CREDITS

Page 9: U.S. Army.

Pages 44, 47, 49, 51: Smoky War Dog LLC.

Page 54: Herson Whitley, with thanks to Mary Ann Whitley.

Page 59: Jennifer Pirante/U.S. Marine Corps.

Pages 63 (bottom), 65: Leslie Reichardt.

Page 73: Robert Throneburg.

Page 77 (bottom): Ken Neal.

Pages 83, 88, 92: John C. Burnam.

Page 94: Linda Hosek/U.S. Army.

Page 98: Reece Lodder/U.S. Marine Corps.

Page 102: U.S. Marine Corps.

Page 108: Michelle Brinn/U.S. Marine Corps.

Pages 114, 117: Gabe to the Rescue.

Page 125: John F. Looney/U.S. Navy.

BIBLIOGRAPHY

Adams, Simon. *Eyewitness World War I*. London: DK Children, 2014.

Adams, Simon. *Eyewitness World War II*. London: DK Children, 2014.

Bidner, Jen. *Dog Heroes: Saving Lives and Protecting America*. Guilford, Conn.: Lyons, 2002.

Bausum, Ann. *Stubby the War Dog*. Washington: National Geographic, 2014.

Bausum, Ann. *Sergeant Stubby*. Washington: National Geographic, 2014.

Bradshaw, John. *Dog Sense: How the New Science of Dog Behavior Can Make You a Better Friend*. New York: Basic, 2011.

Brittain, Vera. *Testament of Youth: An Autobiographical Study Of The Years 1900-1925*. New York: Macmillan, 1933.

Burnam, John C. *A Soldier's Best Friend: Scout Dogs and Their Handlers in the Vietnam War*. New York: Carroll & Graf, 2000.

Burnam, John C. *Dog Tags of Courage: Combat Infantrymen And War Dog Heroes in Vietnam*. Fort Bragg: Lost Coast Press, 2000.

Cummings, Judy Dodge. *Civil War*. Minneapolis: Abdo Group, 2014.

Davis, Burke. *The Civil War: Strange and Fascinating Facts*. New York: Wings, 1996.

Diconsiglio, John. *Vietnam: The Bloodbath at Hamburger Hill*. New York: Franklin Watts, 2010.

Dowling, Mike. *Sergeant Rex: The Unbreakable Bond Between a Marine and His Military Working Dog*. New York: Simon & Schuster, 2011.

English, Tracy L. *The Quiet Americans: A History of Military Working Dogs* (San Antonio: Lackland AFB, 2000).

Frankel, Rebecca. *War Dogs: Tales of Canine Heroism, History, and Love*. New York: St. Martin's Press, 2014.

George, Isabel. *Beyond the Call of Duty*. London: Harper Element, 2010.

Glendinning, Richard and Sally. *Stubby, Brave Soldier Dog*. Champaign, Ill.: Garrard, 1978.

Goodavage, Maria. *Soldier Dogs: The Untold Story of America's Canine Heroes*. New York: New American Library, 2013.

Hamen, Susan E. *World War II*. Minneapolis: Abdo Group, 2014.

Horowitz, Alexandra. *Inside of a Dog*. New York: Scribner, 2009.

Lemish, Michael. *Forever Forward: K-9 Operations in Vietnam*. Atglen, Pa.: Schiffer, 2010.

Lemish, Michael. *War Dogs: A History of Loyalty and Heroism*. Washington: Brassey, 1996.

Millan, Cesar. *Cesar's Way*. New York: Three Rivers Press, 2006.

Niebaum, John H. *History of the Pittsburgh Washington Infantry, 102nd (Old 13th Regiment) Pennsylvania Veteran Volunteers and its Forebearers*. Pittsburgh: Burgum Printing Co., 1931.

Orlean, Susan. *Rin Tin Tin: The Life And the Legend*. New York: Simon & Schuster, 2011.

Pratt, Mary K. *World War I*. Minneapolis: Abdo Group, 2014.

Putney, William W. *Always Faithful: A Memoir of the Marine Dogs of WWII*. New York: Free Press, 2001.

Ritland, Mike. *Navy SEAL Dogs: My Tale of Training Canines for Combat*. New York: St. Martin's Griffin, 2013.

Ritland, Mike. *Trident K-9 Warriors*. New York: St. Martin's Press, 2013.

Robertson, James. *The Untold Civil War: Exploring the Human Side of War*. Washington: National Geographic, 2011.

Rogak, Lisa. *The Dogs of War: The Courage, Love, and Loyalty of Military Working Dogs*. New York: Thorndike Press, 2011.

Ruffin, Frances E. *Military Dogs*. New York: Bearport, 2007.

Selbert, Kathryn. *War Dogs: Churchill and Rufus*. Watertown, Mass.: Charlesbridge, 2013.

Stewart, Alexander M. *Camp, march and battle-field*. Philadelphia: Jas. B. Rodgers, 1865.

Weintraub, Robert. *No Better Friend*. New York: Little Brown, 2015.

Wynne, William A. *Yorkie Doodle Dandy: A Memoir*. Top Dog, 1996.

Zucchero, Michael. *Loyal Hearts: Histories of American Civil War Canines*. Lynchburg, Va.: Schroeder Publications, 2011.

NEWS AND WEB ARTICLES

"AF Sentry Dog To Become Symbol Of Professionalism." Seventh Air Force News, August 9, 1967, tsna.org/7thafnews/aug091967.html. Accessed December 17, 2016.

Alaimo, Carol Ann. "Dogs of war are the most peaceable pooches." *Arizona Daily Star*, January 12, 2004, freerepublic.com/focus/ f-news/1319549/posts. Accessed November 16, 2016.

"Army & Navy - MORALE: Medals for Everybody." *Time*, Feb. 28, 1944, content.time.com. Accessed November 16, 2016.

"Army Dog Is First To Win DSC Award." *New York Times*, Jan. 14, 1944.

"Bin Laden Hunter on Four Legs." *New York Times*, May 4, 2011.

"Cher Ami — World War I Carrier Pigeon." *Encyclopedia Smithsonian,* si.edu. Accessed February 20, 2017.

Collins, Elizabeth M. "Dog, Veteran, Hero." *Soldiers: The Official U.S. Army Magazine*, October 11, 2012, soldiers.dodlive.mil. Accessed November 16, 2016.

Epatko, Larisa. "Military Working Dogs: What Happens After They Serve?" pbs.org/newshour. Accessed November 16, 2016.

Frankel, Rebecca."Military Dogs Sniff Out IEDs, Save Lives." *Wall Street Journal*, October 31, 2014.

"Georgetown Traditions: Jack The Bulldog." hoyasaxa.com/sports/bull-dog.htm. Accessed November 16, 2016.

Hopkins, Kathleen, "Menendez wants to honor 4-legged patriots." *Asbury Park Press*, June 11, 2016, app.com. Accessed November 16, 2016.

Kane, Gillian. "Sergeant Stubby." *Slate*, May 2014, slate.com. Accessed November 16, 2016.

Kelly, Kate. "Chips, First Dog Sent Overseas in World War II." america-comesalive.com. Accessed November 16, 2016.

McBride, Wallace, "Iraq veteran, celebrated working dog Gabe passes away in his owner's arms," *Fort Jackson Leader*, February 21, 2013, army.mil. Accessed November 16, 2016.

McFarland, Cynthia. "Trustworthy Partners." *Ocala Style*, October 28, 2011, ocalastyle.com. Accessed November 16, 2016.

"Old Abe, the War Eagle." Wisconsin Historical Society,- wisconsinhistory.org. Accessed November 16, 2016.

"PDSA Dickin Medal for Lucca." PDSA, pdsa.org.uk. Accessed November 16, 2016.

Scarborough, Rowan. "New law facilitates military dogs return to U.S. adoption by battlefield handlers." *Washington Times*, November 30, 2015.

Sturrock, Staci. "A hero on four legs: Gabe the military dog," *Palm Beach Post*, January 18, 2013, reposted to findagrave.com/cgi-bin/fg.cgi?page=gr&GRid=105204372. Accessed November 16, 2016.

"Tiny War Dog Home...," *Cleveland Press,* December 7, 1945, 1.

Tyson, Peter. "Dogs' Dazzling Sense of Smell." pbs.org/wgbh/nova/nature/dogs-sense-of-smell.html. Accessed November 16, 2016.

"War Dogs of Vietnam," attributed to staff of Hahn AFB, Germany. b-29s-over-korea.com. Accessed November 16, 2016.

Zoroya, Gregg. "How the IED changed the U.S. military." *USA Today,* Dec. 18, 2013.

UNPUBLISHED AND INTERVIEWS

Bahary, Susan. Interviewed by author November 11, 2016.

Reichardt, Leslie, memoir and correspondence. Shared with author.

Throneburg, Robert. Interviewed by author May 24, 2016.

Wynne, William A. Interviewed by author May 25, 2011; February 17, 2016; April 1, 2016.

VIDEOS

CBS. *60 Minutes,* Season 45 Episode 27, April 21, 2013. Video at youtube.com/watch?v=FsnPAQ137fY. Accessed November 16, 2016.

Martin Sheen, narrator. *War Dogs: America's Forgotten Heroes*. Los Angeles: GRB Entertainment Video, 1999.

INDEX

ABOUT THE AUTHOR

Nancy Roe Pimm, a native of Brooklyn, New York, is the author of nonfiction narratives for young readers. Her book *Colo's Story: The Life of One Grand Gorilla* was chosen to represent the state of Ohio at the 2012 National Book Festival, and was a Choose to Read Ohio selection for 2013 and 2014. She is also the author of *The Indy 500: The Inside Track, The Daytona 500: The Thrill and Thunder of the Great American Race, The Heart of the Beast: Eight Great Gorilla Stories,* and *The Jerrie Mock Story: The First Woman to Fly Solo Around the World* (all Junior Library Guild Selections). She lives in Ohio.